W9-CAY-637

This project has been a real joy, thanks to the amazing people at YS. I am grateful to Dave Urbanski for his gracious editing and wonderful humor. Thanks to Jay, Roni, and Mindi for their friendship and guidance. To the YS gang (Jen, Lorna, Dan, Welch, Dave, David, Amy, Andy, Michaela, and Brandi) thank you for your gifts and diligence. Thanks also to Bethel College students Holly Birkey and Tom Carpenter for their contributions. Special thanks to Kelly, my best friend and partner in life, for her editorial reviews and encouragement along the way.

CONTENTS

MIDDLE SCHOOL TALKSHEETS

FOR AGES 11-14

50 READY-TO-USE DISCUSSIONS
ON THE LIFE OF CHRIST

TERRY LINHART

ZONDERVAN®

ZONDERVAN.com/
AUTHORTRACKER
follow your favorite authors

youth
specialties

youth specialties

Middle School Talksheets: 50 Ready-to-Use Discussions on the Life of Christ
Copyright 2009 by Terry Linhart

Youth Specialties resources, 300 S. Pierce St., El Cajon, CA 92020 are published by Zondervan, 5300 Patterson Ave. SE, Grand Rapids, MI 49530.

ISBN 978-0-310-28553-3

Cover design by David Conn
Interior design by Brandi Etheredge Design

Printed in the United States of America

09 10 11 12 13 14 15 16 • 20 19 18 17 16 15 14 13 12 11 10 9 8 7 6 5 4 3

THE HOWS AND WHATS
OF TALKSHEETS

Middle School TalkSheets—The Life of Christ contains 50 discussions that focus on the major events and teachings in Jesus' life…and some that your students may have never encountered before. Each of the 50 discussions includes a reproducible TalkSheet for your students to work on, as well as simple, step-by-step instructions on how to use it. All you need is this book, some Bibles, a few copies of the handouts, and some kids (some food won't hurt, either). Then you're on your way to helping your students discover more about the life of Christ.

These TalkSheets are user-friendly and very flexible. They can be used in youth group meetings, Sunday school classes, or in Bible study groups. You can adapt them for either large or small groups. And they can be covered in only 20 minutes or explored more intensively. You can build an entire youth group meeting around a single TalkSheet, or you can use TalkSheets to supplement other materials and resources you might be covering. This will be a book you'll keep using for many years as you help kids learn more about Christ.

LEADING A TALKSHEET DISCUSSION

TalkSheets can be used as a curriculum for your youth group, but they're designed as springboards for discussion. They encourage your kids to take part and interact with each other while talking about key stories from the life of Christ. And hopefully they'll do some serious thinking, discover new ideas, defend their points of view, and make decisions.

Youth today live in an active world that bombards them with the voices of society and the media—most of which drown out what they hear from the church. Youth leaders must teach the church's beliefs and values—and help young people make the right choices in a world full of options. The stories and themes from the life of Christ are central to helping your middle school students understand their faith.

A TalkSheet discussion works for this very reason. While dealing with the questions and activities on the TalkSheet, your kids will think carefully about issues, compare their beliefs and values with others and with Scripture, and make their own choices. TalkSheets will challenge your group to explain and rework their ideas in a Christian atmosphere of acceptance, support, and growth.

Maybe you're asking yourself, *What will I do if the kids in my group just sit there and don't say anything?* Well, when kids don't have anything to say, a lot of times it's because they haven't had a chance or time to get their thoughts organized. Most young people haven't developed the ability to think on their feet. Since many are afraid they might sound stupid, they often avoid voicing their ideas and opinions.

The solution? TalkSheets let your kids deal with the issues in a challenging but non-threatening way before the actual discussion begins. They'll have time to organize their thoughts, write them down, and ease their fears about participating. They may even look forward to sharing their answers. Most importantly, they'll want to find out what others said and open up to talk through the topics from the life of Christ.

If you're still a little leery about leading a discussion with your kids, that's okay. The only way to get them rolling is to get them started.

YOUR ROLE AS THE LEADER

The best discussions don't happen by accident. They require careful preparation and a sensitive, enthusiastic, and caring leader. Don't worry if you aren't experienced or don't have hours to prepare. TalkSheets are designed to help even the novice leader. The more TalkSheet discussions you lead, the easier it becomes. So keep the following tips in mind when using the TalkSheets as you get your kids talking:

BE CHOOSY

Each TalkSheet deals with a different story from the life of Christ. Choose a TalkSheet based on the needs and the maturity level of your group. Don't feel obligated to use the TalkSheets in the order they appear in this book. Use your best judgment and mix them up any way you want. However, they are roughly arranged in a chronological timeline, so you can focus on a period in Jesus' life, or you can get four or five together for a month's series on a theme or time period.

TRY IT YOURSELF

Once you've chosen a TalkSheet for your group, answer the questions and do the activities yourself. Though each TalkSheet session has a similar structure, they each contain different activities. Imagine your kids' reactions to the TalkSheet. This will help you prepare for the discussion and understand what you're asking them to do. Plus, you'll have some time to think of other appropriate questions, activities, and Bible verses that help tailor it to your kids.

GET SOME INSIGHT

On each leader's guide page, you'll find numerous tips and ideas for getting the most out of your discussion. You may want to add some of your own thoughts or ideas in the margins. And there's room to keep track of the date and the name of your group at the top of the leader's page. You'll also find suggestions for additional activities and discussion questions.

There are some references to Internet links throughout the TalkSheets. These are guides for you to find the resources and information you need. For additional help, be sure to visit the Youth Specialties Web site at www.YouthSpecialties.com for information on materials and other links for finding what you need. Be careful as you use the Internet and videos—you'll need to (carefully!) preview them first (if applicable, you might need to check with your supervisor if you aren't sure if they're appropriate) and try to avoid any surprises.

MAKE COPIES

Your students will need their own copies of the TalkSheet—but make sure you only make copies of the student's side of the TalkSheet. The material on the reverse side (the leader's guide) is just for you. Remember: You're permitted to make copies for your group because we've said you can—but just for your youth group…not for every youth group in your state! U.S. copyright laws haven't changed, and it's still mandatory to request permission before making copies of published material. Thank you for cooperating.

INTRODUCE THE TOPIC

It's important to have a definite starting point to your session and introduce the topic before you pass out your TalkSheets to your group. Depending on your group, keep it short and to the point. Be careful to avoid over-introducing the topic, sounding preachy, or resolving the issue before you've started. Your goal is to spark your students' interest and leave plenty of room for discussion. You may also want to tell a story, share an experience, or describe a situation or problem having to do with the topic. You might want to jump-start your group by asking something like, "What's the first thing you think of when you hear the word _____ [insert the word here]?" After a few answers, you can add something like, "Well, it seems we all have different ideas about this subject. Tonight we're going to investigate it a bit further..."

The following are excellent methods you can use to introduce any lesson in this book—
• Show a related short film or video.
• Read a passage from a book or magazine that relates to the subject.
• Play a popular song that deals with the topic.
• Perform a short skit or dramatic presentation.
• Play a simulation game or role-play, setting up the topic.
• Present current statistics, survey results, or read a newspaper article that provides recent information about the topic.
• Use posters, videos, or other visuals to help focus attention on the topic.

THE OPENER

We've designed the OPENER to be a great kick-off to the discussion. Some may work better to use before you pass out the TalkSheets. Others may work better as discussion starters after the students have completed their TalkSheets. You decide! Check out the MORE section, too—it often contains an alternate opening idea or activity that'll help get students upbeat and talking, which is perfect for leading an effective TalkSheet discussion. TIP: When you're leading a game or OPENER, consider leading it like a game-show host would. Now that may not sound very spiritual, but if you think about what a host does (builds goodwill, creates excitement, facilitates community, listens to others) that sounds pretty pastoral, doesn't it? Plus, it makes it more fun!

ALLOW ENOUGH TIME

Pass out copies of the TalkSheet to your kids after the OPENER and make sure each person has a pen or pencil and a Bible. There are usually four to six discussion activities on each TalkSheet. If your time is limited, or if you're using only a part of the Talk-Sheet, tell the group to complete only the activities you'd like them to complete.

Decide ahead of time if you'd like your students to work on the TalkSheets individually or in groups. Sometimes the TalkSheet will already have students working in small groups. Let them know how much time they have for completing the Talk-Sheet, then again when there's a minute (or so) left. Go ahead and give them some extra time and then start the discussion when everyone seems ready to go.

SET UP FOR THE DISCUSSION

Make sure the seating arrangement is inclusive and encourages a comfortable, safe atmosphere for discussion. Theater-style seating (in rows) isn't discussion-friendly. Instead, arrange the chairs in a circle or semicircle (or sit on the floor with pillows!).

SET BOUNDARIES

It'll be helpful to set a few ground rules before the discussion. Keep the rules to a minimum, of course, but let the kids know what's expected of them. Here are suggestions for some basic ground rules—
• What's said in this room stays in this room. Emphasize the importance of confidentiality. Confidentiality is vital for a good discussion. If your kids can't keep the discussion in the room, then they won't open up.
• No put-downs. Mutual respect is important. If your kids disagree with some opinions, ask them to comment on the subject (but not on the other person). It's okay to have healthy debate about different ideas, but personal attacks aren't kosher—and they detract from discussion. Communicate that

your students can share their thoughts and ideas—even if they may be different or unpopular.

- There's no such thing as a dumb question. Your group members must feel free to ask questions at any time. In fact, since *Middle School TalkSheets—The Life of Christ* digs into a lot of Scripture, you may get hard questions from students that you cannot immediately answer. DON'T PANIC! Affirm that it's a great question, and you aren't sure of the answer—but you'll do some study over the next week and unpack it next time (and be sure to do this).
- No one is forced to talk. Some kids will open up, some won't. Let everyone know they each have the right to pass or not answer any question.
- Only one person speaks at a time. This is a mutual respect issue. Everyone's opinion is worthwhile and deserves to be heard.

Communicate with your group that everyone needs to respect these boundaries. If you sense your group members are attacking each other or adopting a negative attitude during the discussion, stop and deal with the problem before going on. Every youth ministry needs to be a safe place where students can freely be who God created them to be without fear.

SET THE STAGE

Always phrase your questions so that you're asking for an opinion, not a be-all, end-all answer. The simple addition of the less-threatening "What do you think…" at the beginning of a question makes it a request for an opinion rather than a demand for the right answer. Your kids will relax when they feel more comfortable and confident. Plus, they'll know you actually care about their opinions, and they'll feel appreciated.

LEAD THE DISCUSSION

Discuss the TalkSheet with the group and encourage all your kids to participate. The more they contribute, the better the discussion will be.

If your youth group is big, you may divide it into smaller groups. Some of the Talksheets request that your students work in smaller groups. Once the smaller groups have completed their discussions, combine them into one large group and ask the different groups to share their ideas.

You don't have to divide the group with every TalkSheet. For some discussions you may want to vary the group size or divide the meeting into groups of the same sex. The discussion should target the questions and answers on the TalkSheet. Go through them and ask the students to share their responses. Have them compare their answers and brainstorm new ones in addition to the ones they've written down.

AFFIRM ALL RESPONSES— RIGHT OR WRONG

Let your kids know that their comments and contributions are appreciated and important. This is especially true for those who rarely speak during group activities. Make a point of thanking them for joining in. This will be an incentive for them to participate further.

Remember that affirmation doesn't mean approval. Affirm even those comments that seem wrong to you. You'll show that everyone has a right to express ideas—no matter how controversial those ideas may be. If someone states an off-base opinion, make a mental note of the comment. Then in your wrap-up, come back to the comment or present a different point of view in a positive way. But don't reprimand the student who voiced the comment.

AVOID GIVING THE AUTHORITATIVE ANSWER

Some kids believe you have the correct answer to every question. They'll look to you for approval, even when they're answering another group member's question. If they start to focus on you for answers, redirect them toward the group by making a comment like, "Remember that you're talking to everyone, not just me."

LISTEN TO EACH PERSON
Good discussion leaders know how to listen. Although it's tempting at times, don't monopolize the discussion. Encourage others to talk first—then express your opinions during your wrap-up.

DON'T FORCE IT
Encourage all your kids to talk, but don't make them comment. Each member has the right to pass. If you feel that the discussion isn't going well, go to the next question or restate the present question to keep things moving.

DON'T TAKE SIDES
Encourage everybody to think through various positions and opinions—ask questions to get them going deeper. If everyone agrees on an issue, you can play devil's advocate with tough questions and stretch their thinking. Remain neutral—your point of view is your own, not that of the group.

DON'T LET ANYONE (INCLUDING YOU) TAKE OVER
Nearly every youth group has one person who likes to talk and is perfectly willing to express an opinion on any subject—all the time. Encourage equal participation from all members.

LET THEM LAUGH!
Discussions can be fun! Most of the TalkSheets include questions that'll make students laugh and get them thinking, too. Some of your students' answers will be hilarious—feel free to stop and laugh as a group.

LET THEM BE SILENT
Silence can be scary for discussion leaders! Some react by trying to fill the silence with a question or a comment. The following suggestions may help you to handle silence more effectively—

• Be comfortable with silence. Wait it out for 30 seconds or so to respond, which can feel like forever in a group. You may want to restate the question to give your kids a gentle nudge.

• Talk about the silence with the group. What does the silence mean? Do they really not have any comments? Maybe they're confused, embarrassed, or don't want to share.

• Answer the silence with questions or comments like, "I know this is challenging to think about..." or "It's scary to be the first to talk." If you acknowledge the silence, it may break the ice.

• Ask a different question that may be easier to handle or that'll clarify the one already posed. But don't do this too quickly without giving them time to think the first one through.

• The "two more answers" key. When you feel like moving on from a question, you may want to ask for two more answers to make sure you've heard all of the great ideas. Many students have good stuff to say, but for one reason or another choose not to share. This key skill may help you draw out some of the best answers before moving on.

KEEP IT UNDER CONTROL
Monitor the discussion. Be aware if the discussion is going in a certain direction or off track. This can happen fast, especially if your students disagree or things get heated. Mediate wisely and set the tone that you want. If your group gets bored with an issue, get them back on track. Let the discussion unfold but be sensitive to your group and who is or isn't getting involved.

If a student brings up a side issue that's interesting, decide whether or not to pursue it. If the discussion is going well and the issue is worth discussing, let them talk it through. But if things get off track, say something like, "Let's come back to that subject later if we have time. Right now, let's finish our discussion on..."

BE CREATIVE AND FLEXIBLE

If you find other ways to use the TalkSheets, use them! Go ahead and add other questions or Bible references. Don't feel pressured to spend time on every single activity. If you're short on time, you can skip some items. Stick with the questions that are the most interesting to the group.

SET YOUR GOALS

TalkSheets are designed to move along toward a goal, but you need to identify your goal in advance. What would you like your youth to learn? What truth should they discover? What's the goal of the session? If you don't know where you're going, it's doubtful you'll get there.

BE THERE FOR YOUR KIDS

Some kids may actually want to talk more with you about a certain topic. (Hey! You got 'em thinking!) Let them know you can talk one-on-one with them afterward.

CLOSE THE DISCUSSION

Present a challenge to the group by asking yourself, "What do I want my students to remember most from this discussion?" There's your wrap-up! It's important to conclude by affirming the group and offering a summary that ties the discussion together.

Sometimes you won't need a wrap-up. You may want to leave the issue hanging and discuss it in another meeting. That way, your group can think about it more and you can nail down the final ideas later.

TAKE IT FURTHER

On the leader's guide page, you'll find additional materials—labeled MORE—that provide extra assistance to you. Some sessions contain an additional activity—i.e., an opener, expanded discussion, or fun idea. Some have support material that can help you handle some potential confusion related to the topic. These aren't a must, but highly recommended. They let the kids reflect upon, evaluate, dig in a bit more, review, and assimilate what they've learned. These activities may lead to even more discussion and better learning.

A FINAL WORD

My goal in writing this TalkSheet book was to help your students grow in their understanding of the Bible, the richness of the stories from the life of Christ—and to learn more about who Jesus is and his invitation to follow him. The bottom line is to have fun teaching your students from the life of Christ.

1. Imagine your neighborhood or city 100 years from now. Make some predictions about what the following will be like:

Clothes   Cars/Traveling

Church   School

Computers   Space Travel

2. What's the difference between a prediction and a prophecy? Team up with three others and have one person read 2 Peter 1:20-21 from the Bible. As a group, write a sentence that explains what prophecy is.

How is this different from a prediction?

3. There were many prophecies written about Jesus hundreds of years before he was born. Which of the following are the most amazing prophecies that were fulfilled (came true)? Put an "X" next to your top three.

___ His name would be Immanuel.   ___ He'd be born in Bethlehem.

___ Many babies in his town would be killed.   ___ He'd be rejected by his own people.

___ He would enter Jerusalem on a donkey.   ___ He'd be betrayed for 30 pieces of silver.

___ He'd die on a cross between two thieves.   ___ He'd rise from the dead.

4. The people in Israel expected the Messiah because they knew of the prophecies in the Old Testament. Get in groups of three or four, look up the following verses, and write down an answer to each question.

Deuteronomy 18:18—Where would the Messiah come from?

Micah 5:2—Where would the Messiah be born?

John 1:45—How did Philip describe who Jesus was?

Acts 3:18, 22—What did Peter say about Jesus?

5. Rate yourself on the following line.

◄ •• ►

I'm very   I'm sort of familiar   I'm not
familiar with   with the Bible   familiar with
the Bible   the Bible

THIS WEEK

Most middle schoolers are probably unfamiliar with Old Testament prophecies regarding the Messiah. This session exposes students to these key passages of Scripture, shows how the prophecies were fulfilled in the life of Christ, and prompts students to think about the role of Scripture in their lives.

OPENER

Before the meeting, write six questions on a sheet of paper. Make enough copies for everyone. You can make up your own questions or use these six:

1. What will you have for dinner tomorrow?
2. What will the weather be like a week from today? (Be specific with temperature, wind, etc.)
3. What grade will you get on your next test at school?
4. Who will win the next Super Bowl?
5. In 10 years, what will you be doing?
6. In 20 years, what will be a common electronic device that everyone will own? Be creative.

Tell students you're going to have a prediction contest to find out who the best "prophet" is. Pass out the slips of paper and pencils. Play some upbeat background music while students are answering their questions. Have a few students share their answers to questions 5 and 6, making sure you get a wide range of volunteers. Have students put their names on their slips of paper and give them to you. Tell them you'll give prizes to those who gave correct answers for questions 1 through 4, and give those students prizes later. Make sure to follow up on each of these.

DISCUSSION

1. Have your students share some of their predictions.
2. Prophecy comes from God; predictions come from people. The Bible writers were careful to describe a true prophet of God (Deuteronomy 18:22; 2 Chronicles 36:15). Talk through your students' answers and make sure your students understand.
3. Hundreds of years passed between the time these prophecies were written and when they were fulfilled. That's a long time! Though people were very familiar with Old Testament prophecy, do you think it would've been easy or difficult for them to recognize that these were being fulfilled in Jesus' life? Some were able to see these events as the fulfillment of Scripture, but others weren't able to do it.

Why do some people today have trouble believing the Bible to be true?

4. This will take some time, but it will help middle schoolers encounter two prophecies and the responses of some of the disciples as they saw events unfolding in Jesus' life. Peter's summary in Acts 3 happened soon after the resurrection. You may want to write on the board four or five key points from his talk that summarize what he said about Jesus and the gospel.
5. The issue for us is the same as the one faced by those during the time of Christ—we need to be familiar with God's Word, the Bible, to be able to recognize when God is at work in people's lives. In what ways does understanding the Bible help us? In what ways has the Bible helped you? This last one may be difficult for some to answer, but a few students might have some helpful, even amazing answers.

CLOSE

Close by summarizing how prophecy, which was written hundreds of years before Christ was born, was fulfilled. Fulfilled prophecy in the Bible reminds us of its authority in our lives, even though some may choose to ignore it. Following Jesus means we should understand his life and teachings as revealed in the Bible. What commitments can we make to learn more about Jesus and allow him to lead our lives?

MORE

• The Bible can be intimidating for many adults, let alone middle school students. For some the Bible may seem confusing at times, and for others, Bible reading may seem irrelevant to their lives. A youth group can be a great support to introducing students to the Bible. You may want to develop a Bible-reading club in which students encourage each other and discuss their readings with each other online or in informal small groups.

• A fun game to play with some adult leaders is The Swami. One person says he or she can predict the answer to a question that's inside a sealed envelope. Present the envelope to this person. As the Swami holds it to her head, she gives the answer. She then opens the envelope while repeating the answer, and then reads the question inside. Get a group of riddles off the Internet or from a book, pick the five funniest, and use those as your questions. If you play up the dramatic aspects, this can be a lot of fun. Transition out of this by telling students that, though we laugh at this and know it isn't real, some people today put a lot of faith in people who make predictions.

1. When do you pray the best? You know, those times when you pray as if you already know God is listening. Put a "B" (for Best) beside all that apply below. Then go back through the list below and put an "X" beside those times when you don't pray much at all.

THE PRAYER OF A TEENAGER
Mary's prayer
(Luke 1:26-38; 46-55)

____ When I'm hurting   ____ At church

____ When things are going well   ____ Before big events

____ With friends   ____ When I need help

____ In the summer   ____ When I'm joyful

____ During school   ____ For schoolwork

____ With my family   ____ When I'm confident

____ On vacation   ____ When I'm fearful

     ____ Some other time

2. Do you—or does someone in your family—have a regular prayer that's always prayed at meals or at night? If so, write down a few phrases you remember from that prayer:

3. In her prayer, Mary makes some statements about God. Finish each sentence to summarize what Mary meant.

Verse 50—"His mercy extends to those who fear him."   God is _____.

Verse 51—"He has performed mighty deeds with his arm."   God is _____.

Verse 52—"He has brought down rulers from their thrones."   God is _____.

Verse 53—"He has filled the hungry with good things."   God is _____.

4. Mary's response to the angel was simply, "I am the Lord's servant. May it be to me according to your word." Put a checkmark next to the phrase that describes why Mary responded like this:

___ Mary had great trust in God and knew he could do this.

___ Mary had a faith that allowed her to know this was from God.

___ Mary obeyed because she knew this was for real.

___ Mary had a rich prayer life that kept her close to God.

5. Write down the last three times that you've prayed and what you prayed about.

WHEN I PRAYED	WHAT I PRAYED ABOUT
1.	
2.	
3.	

THIS WEEK

Middle school is a time when students can begin to think about prayer and their own practice of it. In fact, some middle schoolers can have well-developed prayer patterns and may not even know it! One of the most beautiful prayers in all of Scripture is the prayer of a teenager, Mary. This TalkSheet exposes students to that prayer and to Mary the teenager, and offers them an opportunity to develop their prayer lives.

OPENER

Before your meeting, copy and enlarge Luke 1:26-38—one for every five students. Cut the verses into strips and put each set into a separate envelope. Keep a bag of candy on hand as a small prize.

Tell students to get in groups of five to six and hand out the envelopes to each group. Each group has the story of the angel visiting Mary, and they need to put the verses in order. The first group to do so will win a fabulous prize (that they will share with everyone else). You may need multiple adult judges available to review the groups' efforts and award a winner. Give the bag of candy to the winning group and encourage them to share!

When finished, read Mary's prayer in Luke 1:46-55 while the students change their posture (from sitting to standing, or from standing to sitting) whenever you read something Mary says about what God has done. After you're finished, ask students how many times they moved during the prayer. *(The answer should be eight.)*

DISCUSSION

1. Read through each of these, asking for raised hands if someone put a "B" next to one and then an "X." Ask them to raise their hands (instead of commenting) so they all can visually contribute to the discussion. Note any relationship between the times when they don't pray much versus when they pray best. Discuss these with students if desired.

2. Is it okay to say the same memorized prayer before each meal, or should people make up a new one spontaneously each time?

3. Note that Mary was strong in her faith in God. This can be seen in her prayer. She shows her knowledge of the Old Testament and of how the Messiah would establish his kingdom on earth. Do any Bible verses affect how your students pray? How did your students learn what to say when they pray?

4. Sometimes it's difficult to trust that God can do big things. Mary knew what God was capable of doing—challenging the rulers of the world and lifting up those who were poor but who trusted in him. Ask students why they think Mary trusted the angel. How would you have responded? Why?

5. Mary's prayer was focused on what God had done and was going to do. Most of our prayers are focused on what we want and on ourselves. One of the truths about prayer is that it can be a meaningful time to experience God's prompting in our hearts—a two-way conversation between friends. Mary's focus on what God is doing is a great example for us in our prayer time—that God wants to work in and through our lives as we spend time with him and allow him to guide us.

CLOSE

Mary's prayer reveals much about her knowledge of the Bible, her awareness of who God is, and her willingness to obey him. Give students time to write out a five-sentence prayer to God on the back of their TalkSheets. Imagine God has just reminded them of who he is in the world and in their lives. What do they need to say to God that they haven't said in a while? Reassure them that no one will read these except them and God. Encourage students to spread out around the room and have music (without words) ready to play in the background. At the end, have students read their prayers silently to God. Close with a prayer for students to reflect the goodness of God and the hope of Jesus Christ in their lives this week.

MORE

• **Consider organizing a prayer emphasis for your youth group over a period of time. Can you organize your group to pray for 24 hours straight? Divide the 24 hours into equal time slots and have them sign up for a time slot. You can host it at your church or building or have students pray at home. If possible, it's best to have it happen at a single location. Some youth groups have held a prayer chain for one week, and other churches have done it for a whole year. You may want to consider a prayer room for the experience where students can write prayers and post them on the wall and read the Bible and prayerful devotional readings. Decorate the room, add some candles, and be creative in putting a vibrant visual emphasis on prayer.**

COMING TO LIFE
The birth of Jesus
(Luke 2:1-17)

1. What were the best gifts you've ever received? Did you receive them for a birthday or for Christmas?

What was the best gift you ever gave someone else?

Look over your answers. What made these gifts the best?

2. The angels first said to the shepherds, "Fear not." Write down your biggest fears:

3. Get with two or three others and have someone in your group read Luke 2:8-14. Imagine you were the shepherds and this happened to you. Write down two or three ways you might have reacted.

4. The Bible says that Immanuel means "God with us." In your group, decide which of the following best describes what that means to you.

___ Because Jesus came to earth, he understands me.

___ When I go through tough stuff, God is with me.

___ God knows me and loves me.

___ God is aware of what's going on in the world.

___ God listens to our prayers and cares about us.

___ Jesus went through the same temptations we do.

5. In verse 14, the angels declare that God offers peace. Look up and read John 14:27. Imagine Jesus is saying this to you. List two or three areas where you'd like to experience God's peace in your life.

THIS WEEK

The birth of Christ is a well-known story, yet it's still worth studying and exploring with middle schoolers. This TalkSheet session exposes students to that story and invites students to experience God's peace through Christ's presence in their lives.

OPENER

Divide the students into four equal groups and tell them you're going to have a Christmas song competition with fabulous prizes for the group that wins. Each group will sing—with all members participating—the first lines from a known Christmas song. Once you, the judge, recognize the song, move to the next group—which then has to sing a different Christmas song. This continues around the circle with each group having to sing a song that hasn't been sung before. A group is out when it can't come up with a song within 15 seconds of its turn beginning, or when the team sings a song that has already been sung. When you're left with one final group, give it a prize they can share with the other groups, like a bag of candy.

DISCUSSION

1. A lot of excitement will be generated as students write down their answers to the first question. Some middle schoolers may have difficulty with the second one (some students won't have had opportunity to give gifts yet or may have trouble remembering a key gift), and that's okay—the focus of the discussion ought to be the final question. List on the board the answers students provide for what makes a gift the best. When finished with this, have someone read Luke 2:1-7.

2. Have fun with this as well. Let students announce their fears. Afterward announce four or five unusual phobias you found online. (Be certain none of your students has any of them!)

3. Quickly get some answers to this question from the various groups. When a group shares, ask a follow-up question to let them explain their answer. You may or may not see a common response. Ask students to tell you how the shepherds reacted. Have everyone look at verse 20 to see how this encounter with Jesus affected the shepherds.

4. The name *Immanuel* was prophesied by Isaiah and can be found in Isaiah 7:14 (also read John 1:14 and Revelation 21:3 for more examples). Just as God heard the cries of the Israelites in Egypt and sent Moses to deliver them out of Egypt, God also responded when he sent his Son, Jesus, to the world. We can trust Jesus and follow him because he has shown us how to live and has given us power over temptation.

5. Peace is a fruit of the Spirit (Galatians 5:22). We can't truly have peace until we're right with God and the Holy Spirit is at work in our lives. The idea of peace is one of freedom from worry. Ask students what role worry plays in the areas they listed. If God is truly with us, should we worry?

CLOSE

Often when we focus on the birth of Christ, we don't see this event and its result as gifts with any immediate effect in our lives. God is with us, and we have Christ's example and words now to understand how to live. Remind students that as they go through the week, God is with them and knows what they're experiencing.

MORE

• **For a bit of fun, play the fabulous game show "Guess Who Wants What Gift?" Give each student a piece of paper on which they're to write their name and the name of a gift they want—something unusual, but something they really want. Do alert them that responses will be shared with the group. Have students fold the papers and hand them to you. Read the responses that grab your attention and have students guess who in their group wants it.**

• **One of the key Old Testament descriptions of the Messiah (Jesus) was that he would be the Prince of Peace (Isaiah 11:1-9). It's rare to hear anyone answer the question, "How's it going?" with "Peaceful." We live in an age that brags about being busy, in which stress seems constant—particularly for middle schoolers. Let students share what they understand about having peace in their lives, which may give you some insight into their world.**

1. What are the traditions or customs in your family? You know…sayings, trips, gifts, habits, routines, etc., that you do regularly just because, well, you've always done them. Write down two or three that are true for your family:

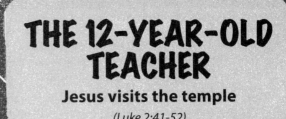

THE 12-YEAR-OLD TEACHER
Jesus visits the temple
(Luke 2:41-52)

2. What's a 12-year-old capable of doing? Put a "Y" next to the activities you think a 12-year-old should be able or allowed to do, and an "N" next to ones you think you can't or shouldn't do.

_____ Drive a car
_____ Teach a lesson
_____ Go on a date
_____ Think of others first
_____ Drink coffee

_____ Have a cell phone
_____ Talk with adults
_____ Solve others' arguments
_____ Be helpful to parents
_____ Go to PG-13 rated movies

_____ Stay up past 10 p.m.
_____ Lift weights
_____ Teach adults
_____ Parachute out of a plane
_____ Love going to church

3. Check out Luke 2:41-50. What was Jesus focused on in this story?

What do you think he was discussing with the teachers?

4. Which of the following best describes Jesus' response to his parents?

_____ I'm God's son, and I want to talk about God's Word.
_____ I'm safe and okay, just where I want to be—in God's house.
_____ You need to remember who my true Father is.

5. Get with two or three others around you, read verses 51 and 52, and write down five things Jesus did as he grew up.

THIS WEEK

One of the few glimpses we get of Jesus' life as a young person is the remarkable scene in which Jesus, at age 12, captivates the teachers in the temple court. This session focuses on Jesus' growth as a young person and encourages students to be examples for others.

OPENER

Divide your group into smaller groups of two to three students each. Have everyone in each group share a story of being really lost. Afterward ask for a few "lost" stories that can be shared with the larger group. Keep it moving, but get two or three good stories. What was the adults' response once they found you? Now, ask the entire group what adults think of middle schoolers. What kinds of things do they say? Do adults say things to them about what they're capable of doing? List students' answers on the board. When you have a good list and feel as though students have shared well, transition into the TalkSheet portion. Tell students you'll be looking at a time in Jesus' early years when he was gone from his parents for a few days and ended up surprising the religious teachers with his knowledge and ability.

DISCUSSION

1. Mary and Joseph went to Jerusalem not because it was a family tradition, but because they were participating in a religious custom or law that was required of every Israelite family—everyone had to attend Passover in Jerusalem (Deuteronomy 16:6). Beyond attending church and youth group, what are the religious traditions for Christians? Would it be a good idea to have more traditions related to being a Christian?

2. Ask your students how they decided which were possible and which were not. List these reasons on a whiteboard as students tell you their answers. Some of them are dependent on laws (like driving) or adults (like movies or cell phones), but some of the answers will center on capabilities. After about two minutes of these, have someone read Luke 2:41-52.

3. Jewish families in that culture and time often traveled in groups, or caravans, with many families together. So it would've been easy for Jesus to be gone a day before Mary and Joseph noticed. Jesus seems to have intentionally stayed behind so he could talk with the teachers of the law at the temple. Give your students a chance to talk about their answers here. Jesus was most likely discussing the Old Testament with the teachers. Can a 12-year-old understand the Bible? The Old Testament?

4. The response of Jesus to his parents shows that, though he grew similar to other 12-year-olds, he was aware of his mission and his relationship to the Father. Ask students why they think his parents didn't seem to understand his character or role.

5. Luke is careful to point out after verse 49 that Jesus was an obedient child and that he grew in four distinct ways. Verse 52 is all that's written of Jesus' life between this moment at age 12, and the beginning of his public ministry at age 30. Have students look over their given areas and then grade themselves on how they're doing in these areas. You might ask them to share how they determined what grade to give themselves.

CLOSE

This scene shows Jesus young, yet deeply committed to God's Word and the Father. When do we talk about God's Word? What do we say when we do? Can middle school students today know a lot about the Bible? Can they be examples for adults? Read 1 Timothy 4:12 and remind students they're in the process of growing, and that they're capable of being strong examples to others—including adults—in what they say, in how they act, and in their commitment to God.

MORE

• **Before the session, draw a circle on a sheet of paper and divide it into four equal quadrants. Label one "social," another "mental," a third "physical," and a fourth "spiritual." Make sure there's room in each quadrant for students to write a few sentences. Make enough copies to give one to each student. Pass them out and have the students reflect on how they're doing at growing in each area. Have them list the people and groups that are contributing to that growth. Are there some areas where improvement is needed? Are there some areas where they don't have support for their growth? What are some steps they can take to grow in these areas?**

1. Which of the following best describe what your church teaches about baptism? (Check all that may apply.)

___ It's an outside sign of something that happened inside a person.
___ It's a first step of obedience that a Christian takes after salvation.
___ It's practiced on babies and is a sign of God's covenant on that person.
___ It's part of what one does to become a Christian.
___ It's done by immersion (being dipped all the way under the water).
___ It's done by sprinkling water on the person's head.

THIS IS GOD'S SON
The baptism of Jesus
(Mark 1:4-13)

2. Team up with someone else and read Romans 6:4. Baptism symbolizes that we've buried our sins from the past and that we're starting a new life as a Christian. Write down a definition of forgiveness:

3. Read Matthew 3:13-14. Then answer these questions:

What does John not want to do?

Why does Jesus want to be baptized?

4. Like a detective, read Mark 1:10-13 and write down a list of what happened.

5. Complete the following sentences.

Others know I'm a Christian because _____.

When I think about baptism, it makes me feel _____ because

_____.

THIS WEEK

Baptism is one of the central practices of the Christian church, yet it's often omitted from Bible studies. There are a range of views on the nature and role of baptism among churches, but it's an important practice in the early church. This TalkSheet gives students an opportunity to learn more about baptism through studying the baptism of Jesus.

OPENER

Ask students if they've ever been part of a club or group (such as a neighborhood club, 4-H, Boy Scouts, Girl Scouts, sports teams) that they had to go through a process to join. Was there an initiation process? What was that like? What initiation processes have they heard about regarding certain clubs? About being in a gang? What does it take to join the church? Do other churches have different processes? Transition into the discussion by telling students that an initiation gives the subject of it the opportunity to be identified with a certain group of people. Have someone read Mark 1:4-13.

DISCUSSION

1. If you're in a church setting, be prepared to let students know what your church teaches about baptism. Each of the possible answers comes from long-standing church traditions of what baptism is. Some of your students may be surprised to see other views listed. It's important to keep students focused on the larger meaning here—that baptism means identification with Christ. Open a discussion over these various answers.

2. How did your students define forgiveness? If we bury something (like garbage), what does that mean? If our sins are buried, how should that affect our lives? 1 Peter 3:21 notes that baptism symbolizes Christ's resurrection and God's forgiveness, allowing us to live with a clear conscience toward God. You may need to define what a clear conscience is and what it looks like in our lives.

3. John wanted to be baptized by Jesus because Jesus was perfect. Point out to students that Jesus was sinless and didn't need forgiveness, but he wanted to be baptized. Jesus, as our Savior, wanted to be identified with humans (Hebrews 2:14).

4. Show students that God showed up on the scene in dramatic ways. God the Holy Spirit appeared in the form of a dove, and God the Father announced (Psalm 2:7) that this was his Son. You may want to discuss what the Holy Spirit does in the lives of Christians.

5. Not all middle school students will be able to answer these two, and that's okay. Students may want to answer the first one with what they've done instead of noting God's forgiveness and the Holy Spirit. Help students see that our good actions are meant to help people see Jesus' example in our lives, not to save us. The last sentence will help you learn more about your students' views on baptism. This is a great opportunity for an informal discussion about baptism and your church's tradition.

CLOSE

Baptism, as a key practice for Christians, is important to discuss today. Jesus, though sinless, was baptized because he chose to identify with us. We're baptized to symbolize our commitment to Christ and to identify ourselves as Christians. Just as Jesus was tempted, we're tempted, too, and need the power of the Holy Spirit to help us live as God wants us to live. Pray for the students that they'll know God loves them, that they'll set a good example for others, and that, as tough times come, they'll choose to rely on God and other Christians and persevere.

MORE

• **Three old TV shows about clubs and initiation may have a scene you could use to kick off your opener.** *Dennis the Menace* **had "Club Initiation" (Season 3, Episode 36, 1962),** *The Andy Griffith Show* **had "Keeper of the Flame" (Season 2, Episode 14, 1966), and** *Diff'rent Strokes* **had "Arnold's Initiation" (Season 8, Episode 12, 1978).**

• **One of the interesting points in the Bible is that baptism is one of the practices that should produce unity among Christians (1 Corinthians 12:13 and Galatians 3:27) since all are identifying with Jesus. You may want to talk with students about how Christians can support each other at school and in neighborhoods. Middle school is a tough time, and many students experience a lot of ridicule and difficulties—and some of it may come from others within their own youth group. Developing a safe atmosphere in your group and among your group members, even while they're away from your group, is a worthy goal.**

1. Rate each of the following middle school temptations using 1 (not very tempting) to 10 (very tempting).

____ Cheating	____ Lying
____ Being proud	____ Drugs
____ Alcohol	____ Being jealous
____ Being too sexual	____ Lusting
____ Smoking	____ Bullying
____ Looking at pornography	____ Wasting time
____ Giving up on commitments	____ Money
____ Eating (too much or too little)	

THE DEVIL IN THE DESERT
The temptation of Jesus
(Matthew 4:1-11)

2. How about you? Put an "X" on the line below that best shows how you respond when facing a temptation.

◄ •• ►

I give in   I'm   I resist
easily   average   easily

3. Read Matthew 4:1-11. Describe in your own words the three temptations Jesus faced:

(1)

(2)

(3)

4. First Corinthians 10:13 says, "No temptation has overtaken you except what is common to us all. And God is faithful; he will not let you be tempted beyond what you can bear. But when you are tempted, he will also provide a way out so that you can endure it." Write down what this verse says about what God has done to help us with moments of temptation:

5. The Bible says that Jesus was tempted in every way (Hebrews 4:15) and yet was without sin. Think about those things that tempt you, but that you know are disobedient to what God wants. Write down two things you need to do when you're tempted by them that will help you resist and take the "way out" that God always provides.

THIS WEEK

Middle schoolers vary in the types of temptations they face based on differences in their parents, friend choices, personalities, media usage levels, and home communities. Some experience a significant amount of temptation, while others are relatively protected. Yet all experience some temptation, and the middle school years are often the first time a student feels the social pull of others. Their choices may produce difficult moments of decision. This TalkSheet will help your group discuss temptations and discover that God can be trusted as they choose to obey him and resist temptations.

OPENER

Tell students that you want to create a definition of the word *temptation*. Write the word on the board and have students describe what it is. Make sure to get a lot of student descriptions and write the key phrases you hear on the board. When you're finished, try to compose a single sentence from most of those phrases.

DISCUSSION

1. This question will reveal much about this issue with your middle school students. You can discover the ratings in a number of ways: You can ask students to share their ratings on each one and see if everyone agrees, or you can actually collect all the numbers and find an average. Which of these are the most common? Do any of these seem like they aren't a big deal?

2. It's important to be careful on this one. You want to both affirm and challenge the students. If a student rates low, they may think they don't measure up to others. But if teenagers think they resist easily, they may be overconfident and unrealistic. You may want students to review their self-rating here and ask if they're being too easy or tough on themselves—and why. Ask students what the danger is in being overconfident when it comes to dealing with temptation.

3. Let students share their answers for this. If these three tests (appetite, selfish gain, power) are the ones we face, what fits under each of them? Put the three tests on the board in three columns. Can your students think of ways middle schoolers are tempted to fulfill a craving? What are some of the ways we're tempted to act selfishly? At home? School? By ourselves? What are ways that middle schoolers try to have power? How about in their friendships? If you're stuck, you may want to go back to question #1 and use those options.

4. Ask for students' answers. As students note God's faithfulness, ask what faithfulness means and help students make some connections to their everyday lives. What is another way to say God will "not let you be tempted beyond what you can bear?" Do your students believe it's true, or do they feel like some pressures are so great that they're overwhelming? If God always provides a way out, what's our responsibility? Discuss it with students, making sure to point out that the verse doesn't say God will take away temptations.

5. The middle school years present new challenges with new temptations—and your kids need to know not just about temptation, but also about recognizing their own struggles and taking action in them. Based on what your students answered, share and discuss tips on how we can all resist temptation. List your students' suggestions on the board. How do they react when they're tempted? Whenever they feel tempted, do they look at ways to get away, or do they feel trapped?

CLOSE

You may want to connect how Jesus was tempted with how Adam and Eve were tempted in Genesis 3:1, 4-5— they all struggled with appetite, being selfish, and gaining power. It might be helpful to show these verses to students and remind them that often our temptations are to satisfy a craving or desire, to be selfish, or to have people like us. You may want to close with a very brief challenge on the concepts of faithfulness or holiness, but always with an acknowledgment of God's grace and forgiveness.

MORE

• **Before doing the TalkSheet, you may want to play "Tempting," an abbreviated version of "Deal or No Deal" or "Let's Make a Deal"—either format would work. You can buy versions of these games online or at a store, but it's best to create your own. Get a variety of suitcases, boxes, or envelopes and put various prizes in them. Include items like youth group T-shirts, coupons for discounts to an event or a local restaurant, and other items—be creative! You can even splurge a bit and put some real prizes in a couple of these. As the host of the game, let students pick an item, but tempt them with another. Once they decide, have a second student play, and so forth. You can have people open their prizes as they go, if you want— just work to create the best tension and the greatest temptation. When finished, pass out the TalkSheets.**
• **Tell students that when we resist the temptation to disobey, we're showing we trust that God's way is best. Close this discussion by giving students a 3 x 5 card and have them write two temptations they face that are difficult to resist. Invite students to commit these areas to God, show their trust that God knows what's best, and nail these to a cross or tear them up and throw them away as a symbol of the victory Jesus offers to us since he also was tempted in every way.**

1. **Which of the following are the most important to you? In each column, select one.**

❑ Clothes   ❑ Friends   ❑ Playing music
❑ MP3, iPod, or CD player   ❑ Teachers
❑ Playing sports
❑ Parents   ❑ Being with friends
❑ Books   ❑ Grandparents
❑ Doing chores   ❑ Video games and system
❑ Neighbors   ❑ Vacations

What is your most prized possession? _____
_____

LEAVING THE NETS
The calling of the disciples
(Mark 1:14-20)

2. Read Mark 1:14-20. If a parent asked you what you wanted to eat for supper, or a friend asked you what you wanted to do, how easy would it be for you to decide? Put an "X" on the line below that shows how easily you make those decisions.

◄ • ►

I make decisions easily   I don't like   Decisions are
       to choose!   difficult for me

3. Team up with one or two others for this one. Jesus says that the kingdom will ask people to repent and believe. For each of these words, write a good definition. If you can, give an example as well.

Repent:

Believe:

4. Jesus told the disciples that if they followed him, they'd be sent out to fish for people. Which of the following do you think best explains what that means?

___ They would help bring people to Jesus so he could heal them.
___ They would be able to learn from him and teach others about Jesus.
___ They would help Jesus become King of Israel and overthrow the Roman army.
___ They could help Jesus get his ministry started and then go back home.
___ They would be empowered to help start the church, which would grow until the end of time.

5. **What are two ways that a middle school student can follow Christ each week?**

THIS WEEK

An important part of Christ's life was his relationship with his disciples—those he invited to follow him and be with him as he taught and healed. This is how we get the image of a Christian disciple being a follower. This account provides a great opportunity to introduce students to the first 12 disciples as well as to the biblical theme of discipleship.

OPENER

To start your discussion time, lead out either with a game of "Simon Says" or a creative edition of "Follow the Leader." Simon Says requires a leader up front who commands and demonstrates various actions, such as "put your right index finger on your nose" for students to mimic. They're only required to do those with the added phrase "Simon Says." The trick for the leader is to get students to perform an incorrect action. The leader does this either by demonstrating something different than the verbal command, or gives and demonstrates a verbal command without adding "Simon Says." Whenever a student performs incorrectly, the student is out and the game continues until only one student is left. Play this at least twice.

"Follow the Leader" can be played two ways. One person can lead the entire group around, or you can divide into pairs and have one person lead the other around. After a few minutes, have players switch. For more variation, have the follower blindfolded.

Have students sit back down and let them discuss what it was like to be a follower during the game. Tell students that this TalkSheet will talk about what it means to be a follower of Jesus.

DISCUSSION

1. If you think it's appropriate, ask students what they checked by reading through each one and having everyone who selected it raise their hands. Ask students to imagine that Jesus asked *them* to lay down one of these for three years and follow him. Which one would be the toughest to lay down? Give 30 seconds for them to circle it. Ask for a few reasons why giving that up would be difficult. Explain that this is similar to what the disciples did when they left their jobs and family business as fishermen.

2. Ask students if it's easy for middle schoolers to make decisions. Do they think it will get easier the older they get? Do some people make decisions better than others? Why? Remind students that the disciples left their jobs "without delay" to follow Jesus. Why did they do that so quickly?

3. Ask students to share one of their definitions that they think is particularly good. "Repent" means to change one's life based on a new understanding of life, sin, and righteousness (Acts 3:19; Romans 10:9-10). "Believe"

means more than just knowing about Jesus (James 2:19), but implies a level of trust that our belief places us in God's care.

4. Discuss with students what they chose and why. The second and fifth answers best reflect what happened. Discuss with students that following Jesus meant trusting him by changing their vocations to being Christ-followers, a choice that would lead to their persecution and—for some—execution for their faith in Christ.

5. A follower begins to look like the person he or she is following. As students share their answers, look for answers that, through those actions, show others who Jesus is. Prompt students to think about two action steps *they* can take to follow Christ this next week. Maybe it's at home, or with friends, or spending time with God in prayer, or learning more about God through reading the Bible. Have them write those steps at the bottom of their TalkSheets.

CLOSE

Tell students that the invitation of Christ is for people to follow him—for *us* to follow him. We do this by trusting that he's the Good Shepherd and has our best interests in mind. Sometimes Jesus asks his followers to leave behind their nets, their goods, and even more to follow him. Ask your students if it's difficult or easy to tell how they're doing at following Christ. Have they ever said to God, "I'll follow you, just as long as I can keep _____?" Close in prayer.

MORE

• The trust issue is a significant one in this topic. When faced with social pressures, academic pressures, family pressures, and expectations from others (like coaches or directors), it's difficult to know how to make decisions. You may want to explore the issue of trust in your students' lives. Do they trust people? Some verses you can give students to look up on trust include Psalm 37:3; 56:11; Isaiah 12:2; and 1 Timothy 6:17.

• For something extra, focus on fishing as an analogy for being a witness. Show an exciting clip of a fishing show (don't laugh—they exist; check out the *In-Fisherman Show* for this) and then ask students how fishing and being a witness are similar. How are they different? If you want students to explore how fishing is used as an example in the Bible, give them these verses: Jeremiah 16:16; Ezekiel 29:4-5; Amos 4:2; Habakkuk 1:14-17; and Matthew 13:47. Have various students read them. How can middle school students be a witness to their friends at school so they can learn about who Jesus is? List the answers on the board and discuss, allowing students to see how they're doing in this area. If you have time, preshoot a video of someone being a witness at school, but shoot it as if it were a fishing show. You may have to watch one to observe the style.

1. Which of the following is the top description of a product labeled "the best"?

_____ Superior to others

_____ Consistent in quality

_____ It gets the job done

_____ Exceeds expectations

_____ Makes me and others happy

_____ Comforting

_____ Changes how I think about it

_____ Is revolutionary and new

WATER INTO WINE
The first miracle at Cana
(John 2:1-11)

2. Write a definition or example for the word *transformation*.

3. Get in groups of three or more, read each of the following passages, and write what they say about how Jesus transforms people.

2 Corinthians 5:16-18—

Ephesians 2:8-9—

4. Stay in your groups and have someone read John 2:1-11. What Jesus did in the story was considered "the best." What are the best ways you reflect who Jesus is? If you can't think of one, what are some best ways you're working on doing this?

5. Look over the following options and check the areas in which you've seen God help you.

____ Relationship with parents

____ Worship

____ Ability to be myself

____ I haven't changed much

____ Other ways

____ Other (list) _____

____ Obeying

____ What I say

____ Dealing with problems

____ My temper

____ Thought life

____ Future vocation

____ Study habits

____ Care for friends

____ Worry

____ Love

THIS WEEK

The first miracle of Jesus took place in what would be a familiar setting—in the midst of people. While attending a wedding of someone who probably knew either Mary or Nathaniel (John 21:2), Mary once again displayed her understanding of who Jesus was by asking him to fix a serious social problem for the wedding hosts. As Jesus took the unclean (the stone jars of water) and made something new and of the best quality, he can do that in our lives, too. This Talk-Sheet provides many opportunities for you and your students to discuss this.

OPENER

Set up four tables around your room ahead of time and have the ultimate taste test of sodas. The cola wars are intense advertising battles, and every student has a favorite, so hype this opening activity before starting it. Set up four tables. On each table, put small sample cups of cola (1), root beer (2), clear soda (3), and some other type of soda (4). Set out as many cups as you have students for each type of drink on each table, making sure to label each cup Type 1, 2, 3, or 4.

Give each student a sheet of paper with four columns labeled "Cola," "Root Beer," "Clear," and "Other," and tell them to go around to the four tables and do taste tests. At each table they're to identify each type of drink and write it down, marking a star next to the one they like best at each table.

If your group is too big for this activity, do it up front and select just three people to come up and compete. After the activity, read off the answers and survey which sodas the students liked best at each table.

DISCUSSION

1. Students may say they want to pick more than once, but have them choose only one. Once everyone has finished, lead a quick discussion on why they chose as they did. After a few minutes, ask the group how they determined which one was best. Tell the group that Jesus' first miracle reveals he was interested in helping create something new in people—something that was best.

2. Allow some students to share their definitions. Write some of the key phrases on the board. Trans-

formation involves an act of changing one thing into another, the new being something with a different composition. Some might call it conversion. It may be interesting to ask students if something can transform itself.

3. Have your students share what they wrote. What does it mean to be a "new creation"? God's workmanship? What is Jesus' job in this transformation process? What is our job?

4. Remind your students that some people see being a Christian as a list of dos and don'ts—versus living the best life. Do your students have a good idea of how a Christian demonstrates God's best?

5. Tell students that this question is about God, not them. Encourage students to let others know what God has done by sharing what they checked. If any want to give a 30-second story about an item, let them.

CLOSE

Read John 2:11 and tell students that this first miracle was one that illustrates both what God can do in our lives—and why. He wants to transform us so that people see our lives and see God's best in action—so that God can get the glory and people will put their faith in Jesus Christ. Have students look over their responses to question #5 and think of ways their life can reflect the best for God this week. After a few moments of silent reflection and prayer, close with prayer for your students.

MORE

• **One of the symbolic elements to this story was the role and use of the stone jars. For other scriptural examples, lead a discussion on 2 Corinthians 4:7-11. What does the stone jar represent? What is the treasure? What is the problem with the jar of clay? Look at 2 Timothy 2:20-23. What does this passage say about what we should do? How do these two passages help us understand what our best should be?**

• **Challenge your students to end each day by reflecting on and writing down what was the best during that day. They can also write down moments where they struggled to show God through how they act. Provide paper for this—paper that looks good with cool fonts and graphics.**

1. **In a typical week in your life, how often do you get angry? Place yourself on the scale below:**

Hardly get angry at all

About once a day

A few times a day

I am regularly angry

How would you finish this statement? When I get angry, it's usually because—

2. Check out Mark 3:1-6. What does Jesus get angry about in this story?

Now read Mark 10:13-16. Who is Jesus upset with here and why?

3. Read Ephesians 4:26-27 and answer the following questions: Is it okay to get angry? Why?

What should a Christian be quick to do when he or she is angry?

What's the danger in staying angry for a long time?

4. Next to each of the following, put "A" if you agree and "D" if you disagree with the statement.
____ A person should never admit to being angry.
____ Anger is best handled by ignoring it or keeping it inside.
____ Angry feelings usually go away if you don't deal with them.
____ Anger is best expressed freely and quickly.
____ Anger is a part of life, but forgiveness must quickly follow.

5. How can we learn to handle anger effectively?

9. JESUS AND ANGER—The temple is cleansed *(John 2:13-17)*

THIS WEEK

Anger and adolescence seem to go hand in hand. Everyone experiences anger. It's not always wrong to be angry, but anger is the cause of many other problems that can plague people. This scene in the life of Christ provides a rich opportunity to discuss when and why Jesus got angry and to examine Bible verses that deal with anger. Students will be able to examine their anger in light of Christ's example.

OPENER

Welcome students to a Things That Really Bug Us support group. Tell them they need to support each other as they put up with annoying things in life. Have students team up with one or two others and share some things that really bug them at home, school, with food, or with friends. After three or four minutes, ask for some unusual examples. This should be fun, with lots of laughter. Let students share what bothers them freely and quickly. Feel free to ask students to clarify or explain. Have a good story ready about your own most unusual pet peeve to close this out. Tell students these things are often called "pet peeves" and transition into the discussion by working on a group definition of a pet peeve, which you can write out on the board. When finished, tell students that today's story focuses on a moment when Jesus got angry, and lead them to use that to think about what *they* get angry about.

DISCUSSION

1. This first question moves past pet peeves to anger. Based on their answers, what did students notice about themselves and anger? Go through the reaction list and ask students to raise a hand to show which options they chose. Ask, "Was it easy or difficult to be honest about getting angry?" Tell students that most people usually get angry when they feel unaccepted, ignored, controlled, or when they're thinking selfishly. Go over those four items again with students and ask which of the four is most common for middle schoolers.

    If it's difficult for students to share out loud about anger, keep moving toward the story by reading John 2:13-17. What was Jesus upset about in this story? How do you know Jesus was upset? The people were selling animals for sacrifices and exchanging money with pilgrims—activities that became less about ministry and more about making big profits.

2. Do you notice a pattern in when Jesus gets angry and at whom? Jesus demonstrates his anger with people who say they're religious but don't act that way—people who don't show a love for God and who even keep others from experiencing God's love. What was Jesus' response to sinners around him?

3. Do your students think it's okay to get angry? After some discussion of these questions, tell students that the key is to be angry only about issues God gets angry about—and that's the problem. We usually get angry for selfish reasons. So we need to deal with it as this passage indicates—by settling our anger quickly with forgiveness and not letting it become wrath or develop into bitterness.

4. Go through each one and ask students to raise their hands to indicate their answer. The first four are incorrect statements about anger, yet they're common ways that many people deal with anger. If these are incorrect, how is it that we learn to handle anger in these ways?

5. What role does forgiveness play in dealing with anger? Is it easier to ask for forgiveness or grant forgiveness? Are there people with whom you're still angry—people you need to forgive? Bring a pillow to the meeting. Ask students which they would pick for a playful fight with a friend: Baseball bats or pillows? Get the pillow out and ask how a pillow can serve as a good example of how people should treat friends, family, and others. What did they write down that can help soften their angry moments?

CLOSE

Read James 1:19-20 and tell students that—though anger is part of being human—we're told to be slow to become angry. Most people get angry about issues very different from the kinds of things that angered Jesus. Remind students that Jesus modeled righteous anger for us and that he invites us to follow him. Even as he hung on the cross, he still modeled forgiveness and grace.

MORE

• To help your students work on anger, Les Parrot suggests having students keep a Hassle Log for a week in which they can record the moments when they got upset. Have them create different columns to note the place, what happened, the person or people, what the person said or didn't say, and the student's response. For a positive addition, suggest using half the sheet as a Blessing Log where students can record moments when they were blessed. This helps students see not only what's going wrong, but also what's going well.

• Anger is so common, but amazingly, it can be a topic that doesn't grab students in a youth ministry setting. To overcome this, create one or two role-play situations in which middle schoolers might commonly get mad. Write a paragraph that sets the scene and short descriptions of each character. You may want one scene set at home and one with friends. Select students or adults who can act well and let them look at the scenes beforehand. After the role plays are performed, lead a short discussion that first allows students to report what they noticed and then enables them to make connections to anger in their own lives.

28   L E A D E R ' S   G U I D E

1. Which of the following is most true about you (circle one)?

I like to be open and honest

I just take life as it comes

I like to be sneaky

2. What do some of your friends misunderstand about what it means to be a Christian? Check all that are true.

❑ It's just a bunch of rules.
❑ You're a Christian if your parents are.
❑ Everyone is a Christian already.
❑ It's boring and you can't have fun.
❑ You have to look sad to be a Christian.
❑ Jesus isn't the only way to God.

MIDNIGHT MEETING
Nicodemus visits Jesus
(John 3:1-21; 7:50-51; 19:38-40)

3. Read John 3:1-3. Nicodemus came to Jesus in the middle of the night. Why do you think this religious leader did that? Check as many as you think apply.

____ It was the only time he could meet Jesus since he worked in the daytime.
____ He was afraid of being seen by others.
____ He didn't want any interruptions.
____ He wanted to have a private conversation with Jesus.

4. Read John 3:16-17 and then answer the following:

What does verse 16 say about what God did?

What does verse 17 say about why Christ came into the world?

Now, read verse 21. What does this verse say about our actions?

5. So what did Nicodemus do? Get with someone near you. Have one person read John 7:50-51 and the other John 19:38-40, and write down what happened:

6. Choose at least one thing you truly need to do this week.

____ I need to get with a Christian adult and talk about some stuff in my life.
____ I need to continue to be confident that Jesus is who the Bible says he is.
____ I need to give my heart and life to God for the first time.
____ I need to be careful how I act so others will know I'm a Christian.
____ I'm not sure what I need to do.
____ I need to ask forgiveness for my sins and recommit my life to Christ.
____ (Other) _____.

THIS WEEK

Middle schoolers have natural curiosity, and the story of Nicodemus shows that people in Jesus' time were curious about who Jesus was, too. It's important *not* to assume that students understand the gospel message and how Jesus' life, death, and resurrection was a new thing to those in Bible times—a work full of God's grace, love, and truth. This TalkSheet tells the story of Nicodemus, a secret follower of Christ, who came to Jesus in the night to learn more about what it meant to be a Christ-follower.

OPENER

Have students stand. You're going to give them some activities, and they're to decide whether it's better to do that activity at night or in the daytime. Designate one side of the room "daytime" and the other "nighttime." Ask students to move to one side or the other based on their decision. Announce these activities one at a time and let students move to designate their choice (perhaps have a morning section just for fun). Activities: Telling ghost stories, mowing the yard, hunting, going on a date, reading your Bible/doing devotions, IMing with friends, doing homework, sneaking around, shopping, going to a movie, or talking about God.

Let your teens know that today's story takes place at night. The darkness of night was an important illustration for the writer as he told the story of Nicodemus. Nicodemus was an important religious ruler who became a secret follower of Christ—and it all started with a midnight meeting to learn more about who Jesus was.

DISCUSSION

1. Ask for a show of hands for each item. If you have a sneaky story from your past that you can tell in two minutes, you might want to share that here. Ask if it's ever okay to be sneaky. When isn't it okay?
2. Find out what answers your middle schoolers chose. Have any of your students tried to correct these with their friends? Which of these might some Christians think are true? Can you see how any of your friends might see some of these as accurate? For instance, are Christians more joyful than others?
3. All of these answers are possible reasons. No one knows why Nicodemus came to Jesus at night, but John uses nighttime as a symbol later in the passage. In John, Jesus is shown as the light of the world (John 8:12), and those who don't believe in him are described as being in spiritual darkness (John 3:19-22). Ask students if they ever got scared at night as a kid. Why did that happen at night and not in the daytime? Ask if they think there's more evil at night than in the daytime. Do people usually act differently at night than in the daytime? Tell students that in John 3, the phrase "born again" also means "born from above." Which one best describes what it means to become a Christian?
4. Go over these three verses, soliciting answers from your students. Write them on the board with verse 16 at the top,

17 in the middle, and 21 at the bottom. Be sure to point out that God gives us a new start and a new nature. What does it mean to condemn? Why is it good that God didn't come to condemn us? When we put our faith in Christ, we're not only forgiven from the past, but we're also given a new nature powered by the Holy Spirit (2 Corinthians 5:17). Remind students that Jesus came into the world to save the world because of God's great love, but that there's also a judgment of those who don't believe. Still, Jesus' desire is that people put their faith in him (John 5:24).
5. Let students share their answers. Nicodemus defended Jesus in front of the other Pharisees and was ridiculed for it. He aided in the burial of Jesus, bringing a generous amount of burial spices, a scene also set at night. Ask students whether or not they think Nicodemus became a follower of Christ in light of these actions.
6. Encourage your students to follow through on whatever they feel they need to do. They may want to change their answer after the discussion. Let them know they can talk or pray with someone if needed.

CLOSE

Point out that Nicodemus' visit to Jesus at night was an illustration of a choice that we have: To live in darkness or to live in the light. Living in the light means more than just being good. It begins by believing in Jesus Christ (verse 16) and choosing to obey him with your whole self (verse 21). Read John 1:12 to your students and connect being called "children of God" to Jesus' teaching that we can be "born from above." Because we are God's kids, so to speak, it's our job to obey God—it shows we love him (John 14:15) and trust that his way is best. Be sensitive to where your students are. Depending on how this discussion went, you may want to close with an invitation for students to respond, or just close with prayer.

MORE

• **One of the subjects this passage can raise is that of baptism. Though various denominations practice it differently, baptism is a central practice for Christians (Matthew 28:18-20; Acts 2:41). Jesus' use of the word *water* in verse 5 has been interpreted differently by different denominations. It was used here in a way Nicodemus could understand, so it either referred to John the Baptist's ministry (Matthew 3:1-6) or the Old Testament's teaching regarding the cleansing power of the Spirit of God (Ezekiel 36:24-27). The latter seems to fit better because other parts of the New Testament also show a connection between water and the Spirit (Titus 3:5).**
• **The old-but-good song "In the Light" by dcTalk connects well to this session. Find the lyrics at www.christianlyricson-line.com/artists/dc-talk/in-the-light.html. Also find a video of the song at www.youtube.com/watch?v=BtxmRdRG0m0, or find the song on the available concert video, *Welcome to the Freak Show*. Show the lyrics while you play the song, and discuss with students what problems the song discusses. What's the solution? Connect that to the story of Nicodemus and John 3:21.**

1. **Are there certain kinds of people that just kind of bug you? Put a checkmark next to the three that are most annoying to you.**

___ Bossy people	___ Quiet kids
___ Messy people	___ "Neat freaks"
___ Short or tall people	___ Skinny or heavy people
___ Older people	___ Immature elementary kids
___ People who talk too much	
___ People who dress weird	
___ People with different skin color	
___ Musical people	___ Good athletes
___ Smart people	___ Other (describe)
	_____

> # CROSSING BARRIERS
> ## Jesus with the woman at the well
> *(John 4:1-42)*

Do you make fun of anyone? Put a circle around one or two types of people in the list above that might be the kind of person you'd tease.

2. **Why do kids pick on or ignore others at school?**

3. **Read John 4:7-15. List at least two ways the people in this story are different from each other.**

4. **What do you think Jesus means by "living water"?**

5. **Read John 4:39-42. What was the result of Jesus stepping across a barrier and revealing who he was to those who were being put down?**

Write down the first names of two people who are put down by others. List one or two ways you can show who Jesus is to each of them.

THIS WEEK

The story of Jesus' encounter with the woman at the well has been seen as either a model for relational evangelism, or a model for multicultural ministry. Middle school is a period where differences make kids into targets of ridicule, and they may endure repeated teasing and bullying for a variety of reasons—clothing, appearance, comments, hobbies, anything. Even your students go along with the crowd to fit in by joining in the teasing of those who are different. A kid can talk about loving God one night and the next day act very differently. This TalkSheet focuses students' attention on social barriers that separate us, but that need to be crossed in order to show Christ's love to others.

OPENER

What do people pick on or tease each other about at school? Ask students to shout out some answers while you write them on the board. Discuss with your students: What's the purpose or goal of teasing? Does it ever go too far? Ask students to raise their hands if they've ever been picked on to the point that it really hurt, even if no one really knew that it did. How did they cope with that? Discuss with students how the kids at their school are divided into various groups. How did your students decide which group to belong to? Are they aware that they're in a group, or not?

Tell students that today's story focuses on a scene where Jesus ministered to a woman and her friends in an area (Samaria) that was home to people who were considered outcasts. Samaritans were repeatedly ignored and picked on, but Jesus provided a model to follow if your students want to be an encouragement to others.

DISCUSSION

1. Go through these quickly and have students raise their hands for the ones they picked. Keep an eye out for the four or five items that get the most votes. After finishing the votes, go back and ask why those are the most annoying. Push a bit, and transition to how those people are treated. Remind students that people are watching them to see if their relationship with God makes a difference or not—and the *first* place they look is at how your students treat others.

2. Try to push a bit here, too. What's the purpose of teasing or putting others down? Is it just something people do? Does it make people look better when they slam someone else? Ask them how they feel when it's happening to *them* and let them share a bit. Then, gently (gently!) remind them that some of them treat others that way. They may sing about how much God loves everyone at church, yet be just like everyone else the next day at school.

3. Tell students Jesus crossed many barriers that separated people. First, as God, he showed that God has come to us—we don't have to try to get up to him. Even though we sinned and wronged him, he loves us so much that he meets us where we are. Second, as a Jewish man, he was very unusual for talking to or associating with a Samaritan. Jesus

was mocked by being called a Samaritan in John 8:48. Further, the Samaritans were seen as unclean—to ask to drink water from a Samaritan's jar, especially a woman's, would've been unthinkable. Have students look at verse 27 to see the disciples' reaction when they saw Jesus doing this.

4. Ask for student responses. Some will point to Jesus' use of an object lesson, since they were at a well. There were some Old Testament Scriptures Jesus might have been referring to, such as Jeremiah 2:13. Why didn't Jesus just tell the woman clearly who he was?

5. This gives you a chance to talk about being a witness to others. Do your students talk to others about their relationship with Christ? Do they pray for opportunities to be a witness? Do they invite others to come with them to your group? These are key practices for students who want to be a witness to others. Ask students to share the ways they plan to show love to others. You can list them on the board to show your kids how they'll be showing love to others over the next few weeks.

CLOSE

Summarize the story by reminding students that the story begins, "Now he had to go through Samaria" (verse 4). Most Jews avoided this route through Samaria and instead crossed the Jordan River to avoid the Samaritan people. So why did Jesus decide to go through Samaria? Jesus had an appointment with a Samaritan woman that was important for his disciples and for the village to see (verses 27 and 29-42). The early ministry of the church was to include the Samaritans (Acts 1:8 and 8:48). So what are the areas that we may *have* to go through to be obedient to God? Close with prayer for your group to follow Christ's example in this story and for the courage to follow the steps students have written down for the last question.

MORE

• **A key problem in many groups is that students don't support each other throughout the week at school. In fact, some of the kids in your group may actually be picking on other kids in your group. This TalkSheet is a great opportunity to talk about the community of the group. You can go at this a number of ways. Make a group covenant for how the students will treat each other outside of meeting times, or pass out 3 x 5 cards and have students anonymously share how *they're* doing in this area. Do they feel supported by others in the group? Are they being picked on or bullied at school?**

• **You may want to focus on the barriers that divide people and ask students to identify these social barriers. You may need to prompt your students to think about how students divide by gender, by color of skin or ethnicity, and so on. How about by wealth? Is this a bigger deal in high school? You may want to check out some resources on racism and social class. There are many good resources through Youth Specialties or urban networks. Efrem Smith wrote on racism and used John 4 at www.youthspecialties.com/articles/topics/urban/passion.php.**

1. What three words would you use to describe your hometown to someone else?

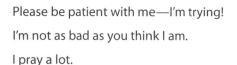

2. Do adults misunderstand middle schoolers? Put a "Y" next to any of the following you'd like to say to your parents, teachers, coaches, or church leaders.

Thanks for spending time with me.

I try to do my best in everything.

I'm enjoying my life.

I'm okay, just having fun with friends.

I am really hurting now, but can't talk about it.   Please be patient with me—I'm trying!

Please listen to my point of view.   I'm not as bad as you think I am.

I "get" God more than I show on the outside.   I pray a lot.

Please don't think I'm out of control.   I can work hard if I want to.

3. Look up and read Mark 6:1-6. Write down what the people in Jesus' hometown said about him.

Luke tells part of this story in Luke 4:28-30. Read those verses. If you were a reporter there, what would your headline be for your newspaper article?

4. In Mark 6:6, what amazed Jesus?

5. Imagine that one of your friends asks you to explain what it means to put faith in Jesus Christ. Look up John 12:44-46 and Romans 10:9-10 and write an explanation for your friend.

THIS WEEK

Jesus spent almost 30 years as a carpenter's son in Nazareth, looking a lot like all the other boys. After his baptism, Jesus began his ministry of teaching, healing, and gaining a reputation among the people of the region. This TalkSheet focuses on Jesus' return to his hometown, where it was difficult for those who knew him to understand what was happening. At one point in the synagogue, he read from the prophets about the Messiah—and then made the bold statement that he fulfilled those prophecies. What a moment that must have been for those watching! This TalkSheet connects the themes from this dramatic story to the lives of middle schoolers and helps them reflect on their own response to who Jesus is.

OPENER

Divide your group into equal groups of six to 10 students and tell them you're going to play the incredible game show called Guess Where You Are! Get students clapping as if they're a game show audience. An "APPLAUSE" sign might help. Before the meeting, go around your city or area and take lots of digital pictures of different spots. Pick the best 10 photos and make a computer slideshow. Give your teams a sheet of paper with numbers 1 through 10 on it and tell students to write down where the picture was taken. (You can see you'll want to be creative with your picture taking and have various levels of difficulty). After you go through the 10 pictures, go back through them and give the answers. Have teams check off the number they got correct and give a small prize to the team with the highest score.

Transition by explaining that this TalkSheet focuses on a key scene in Jesus' early ministry. Jesus returns to his hometown, Nazareth, and has a dramatic teaching moment in the synagogue. The townspeople responded in anger and tried to kill Jesus, but the scene also shows us what Jesus said about his ministry.

DISCUSSION

1. Have students quickly share their words. There'll be some funny and unusual responses. Ask for further reasons and examples as desired. This needs to be upbeat for your whole group, so keep it fast-paced and use it to draw out some students who may not normally share.

2. Though your students may have marked some of these, a few are too personal or embarrassing for students to discuss—so be sensitive. Discuss what they would let adults know about middle school students. Move quickly to the question, "What do adults misunderstand about middle schoolers?" and generate a list from students' responses. Remind students that Jesus had grown up in Nazareth, so when he began to teach

and do miracles, it was difficult for people to accept what was happening—and especially to accept who he was.

3. Ask some students to share their headlines and use these to help students understand the scene. You may want to have someone read Matthew 13:53-58 and Luke 4:16-30 before leading this discussion.

4. Jesus observed a lack of faith in his hometown. What *should* we believe about Jesus? You can make a list on the board, a chance to teach your middle schoolers a good theology of who Jesus is. You may want to do some study on this before the TalkSheet so you can take advantage of this opportunity.

5. Ask students to share their explanations. Did any of them include ideas that connect to Jesus' helping us see or to coming out of the darkness? If not, make sure to discuss that comparison. Finish this question by discussing what *our* response should be. You can go one step further and ask students to think through what their response to Christ has been.

CLOSE

You may want to close by reading Isaiah 61:1-2, the section Jesus read from in the Luke 4 account. Tell students that Jesus' ministry was going to be about saving people—from poverty, from being bound as a prisoner to sin, from being oppressed, and from spiritual blindness.

You may want to talk to your students about the pressures they face that keep them from being who God made them to be. It's not uncommon for a middle school student to feel overwhelmed by problems or pressures or to feel confused about spiritual topics. Remind students that the power to overcome is not our own strength, but our faith in Jesus—these promises are what God does. Close by talking about the kind of response God wants from us.

MORE

• **This Bible story is shown on the DVD *Jesus of Nazareth*. The movie expands some themes, but the core message is still present. Use it to set the tone for the significance of Jesus' words—how people knew he meant that he was the Messiah. You can also find the clip from the movie online on YouTube.com.**

• **Remind students that there are remarkable people in your youth group, but that we usually don't spend time recognizing that. Rather, we pick on or make fun of others instead of choosing to see what God sees. You may want to try a group affirmation exercise in which everyone writes affirming sentences about others on a sheet of paper. You'll need to create these so that each student writes his or her name at the top of the sheet. Then have students pass them around so others can write affirmations. At the end, pass the sheets back to the students so they can read the affirmations about themselves.**

1. **What animal best describes your personality?**

_____

What's your best quality? _____

Fill in these blanks:

_____, the _____,
     (your name)   (the animal like you)

champion of _____.
          (your best quality)

Team up with one or two others and, for each of the following snapshots, read the verses for each and answer the snapshot question in each frame.

FOLLOW THE LEADER
The disciples
(Matthew 10:2-4; Mark 3:16-19: Luke 6:12-16)

---

2. James and John (nicknamed by Jesus "sons of thunder," Mark 3:17)
Read: Mark 10:35-37, 41; Luke 9:54.
What was their desire?

How might their nickname have been true about how they acted?

---

3. Andrew
Read: John 1:40-42; 6:8-9; 12:21-23
What is Andrew doing in each of these three stories?

If Andrew was at your school or in your youth group, what might he spend time doing with his friends?

---

4. Nathanael
Read: John 1:45-49
What kind of response did Nathanael give Philip?

How did Jesus deal with Nathanael?

---

5. Thomas (also called Didymus)
Read: John 20:20-28
Why did Thomas doubt?
What was his response after seeing Jesus?

Read: John 11:14-16 and 14:5-6. What kinds of personality traits are seen here? How might those contribute to doubt?

---

6. **Which of these four snapshots seem most like you? Why?**

THIS WEEK
The 12 disciples who followed Jesus were the main focus of Jesus' ministry. Invited to follow him, they came from a variety of backgrounds and had their share of struggles along the way, but they eventually helped launch the church after Pentecost. This TalkSheet introduces your middle schoolers to the various disciples and, through focusing on five of them, helps students identify with them.

OPENER
Give everyone a 3 x 5 card and ask them to write their names at the top of the card. Have them write any nicknames they've been given. They can write more than one. Make sure they write clearly and use appropriate nicknames! Collect the cards, read out the nicknames, and see if people can guess who it is. Without embarrassing anyone, you can occasionally ask for the story of how someone received a particular nickname. You want to celebrate who your students are! Were there any based on personality or actions? Were any nicknames about a physical feature (hair, height, and so on)? When finished, ask what the purpose of a nickname is. Why can't people just call each other by their real names? Do any of your students hate one of their nicknames?

DISCUSSION
1. Ask them to share their titles. This is how some names were given years ago. What did you learn about some of your friends? Have any of your students had a picture of them that perfectly captured who they are?
2. James and John didn't understand what kind of kingdom Jesus would be ruling. They wanted to be great and respected, which might come from being in a wealthy family with hired servants (Mark 1:20), but not from Jesus' kingdom. What kind of personalities do wealthy people have? Do people act like this today? How? Do middle schoolers?
3. Each time we see Andrew, he's bringing someone to Jesus. Why did he do that? In what ways was Andrew an encourager to others? How should we be an encourager to others?
4. Tell students that Nathanael's sarcastic comment showed his disrespect of Nazareth and his limited view of what God could do. Once Jesus demonstrated his supernatural ability, Nathanael's response showed his knowledge of the Old Testament and his understanding of who Jesus was. Is it okay to be sarcastic?
5. Remind students that Thomas' encounter with Christ shows his doubt and lack of trust. How does fear cause someone to doubt? Thomas was pessimistic

(make sure your students know what that means) and thought things weren't going to go well. How does being scared about the future hurt someone's ability to trust God?
6. Note that it's encouraging to see that the Bible has many normal, imperfect people who show us the result of God's ability to transform people. Despite their struggles and hesitation, God used these disciples and the others to spread the gospel and help start the church. It's easy to get discouraged about what we do wrong, and sometimes it's difficult to think God could use us for something great. Ask students which of these disciples they're most like. Build from that to point out or discuss ways in which their personalities affect their relationship with God.

CLOSE
Remind students of the importance of remembering that God is the one who changes us. While we need to do our part in praying and reading the Bible, God is the one who can take regular people with regular personalities and habits, and do great things. The disciples found out who Jesus was and trusted him, but didn't always get it right. However, once they let the Holy Spirit lead them, they were strong witnesses of what God can do. Discuss with your students what it means to be committed to God as a middle schooler and how God wants to use them, even with their regular personalities, to show others the difference Jesus makes.

MORE
• Create "disciple snapshots" of your students before the meeting. A week or two before, use a digital camera to take pictures of your students and print them on 8 x 11 papers so that each student has his or her own page. Make two columns under each photo, the first titled "What I'm like" and the other "What God is doing in my life." Pass them out to the students and have students fill them out. After about four minutes, allow students and adults to walk around and add their observations and thoughts to the papers of others. Make sure you write positive comments that reinforce the good things you see in each of your students. Before the day of your TalkSheet session, write a comment yourself for every student to save time and set a positive tone.
• If you want, you can build off this in two directions. First, find materials on spiritual gifts or personality types and show students the range of spiritual gifts that exist. Most tests are adult-oriented, so it's not appropriate to give one to middle schoolers. But you could discuss what a spiritual gift is and let students help you define the word *disciple*. The word is used often in the Gospels and in Acts, but not in Paul's writings. What do your students think of when they hear the word? How is a disciple a learner? A follower? An imitator? A brother or sister? What other analogies can your group think of for the word *disciple*?

1. Do you "A" (agree) or "D" (disagree) with the slogans below?

____ People can find out who Jesus is without help from others.

____ God helps those who help themselves.

____ We have to be careful how we talk to others about God so we don't turn them off.

____ I need my friends to help me in my relationship with God.

> # CARRYING FRIENDS TO JESUS
> ## The man let down through the roof
> *(Luke 5:17-26)*

2. Read Luke 5:17-26. Imagine you're creating a short movie about this story. Pick the most powerful scene.

❏ The friends trying to get through the crowd.
❏ The friends tearing up the roof.
❏ The sick man being lowered down in front of Jesus.
❏ The Pharisees angry with Jesus.
❏ Jesus' response to them—healing the man.
❏ The man standing up and the crowd's amazement.

How would you shoot it to capture the best emotional qualities?

What music would you use?

3. Imagine that you are in this story. Who best represents your situation? Put an "M" next to the one most like you, an "S" next to any you're sometimes like, and an "N" next to any you're never like.

The man on the mat in need of Jesus.

The Pharisees, confused about who Jesus is.

The friends carrying the man, helping their friend find Jesus.

The crowd, watching what's going on.

4. Jesus first forgave the man before healing him. It's easy to create a wish list of things we'd like to change about ourselves physically. But if we were to create such a list of spiritual changes, what two or three would you like?

____ I could have more faith.

____ I could help others find Jesus.

____ I would understand the Bible better.

____ I would be a better example with others.

____ I would know God's will for my life.

____ I wouldn't be as critical.

____ I would know that God loves me.

____ I would get closer to Jesus.

____ I would pray better.

____ I wouldn't be as fearful.

____ God would forgive me.

____ (Other) _____

THIS WEEK

One of the great responsibilities your middle schoolers have is to let their lives be an example to others of who God is. Sometimes when friends have problems or are in need of guidance, that isn't enough. Action is needed to get them to see who Jesus is and how he can help them. There were some friends in the Bible who did this. They had a friend in need of healing and they weren't going to be easily blocked from getting him to Jesus.

OPENER

Gather the following items beforehand and give one to each group so each group has a different item—a medicine bottle (empty of meds, but you can put in some jelly beans), a piece of exercise equipment, a full bottle of a sports drink, a trendy clothing item, a magazine ad for a vacation spot, a common small kitchen appliance, and other similar items. Divide the students into groups of six or so and tell them they're to create and perform a commercial for a product that will solve everyone's problems. Give the groups five minutes to come up with a 30-second commercial and have each group perform its commercial. Afterward, discuss what claims each group made about their product's power. Do people really trust that these products will solve problems in their lives? Are there other ways people try to be healed from problems? The focus of this Talk-Sheet is on some friends who had faith that Jesus could heal one of their friends, and they took dramatic action to get him to Jesus.

DISCUSSION

1. Discuss with your students ways that people who don't know anything about God can learn more about Jesus Christ and eventually commit their lives to him. You may want to list these on the board. What are some problems with the phrase "God helps those who help themselves"? Do your students think they have to be careful in what they say to friends about God?

2. Which scene is the most dramatic? Couldn't all of them be produced in a dramatic way? You may have an idea for how each of the scenes would make a great movie scene. Now have your students think about which scene in their lives would be the best to show what God has done in their lives. Would it be a scene at church, something at school, a sum-

mer camp, or a time alone with God? Your students may not be able to share about this, so be quick to talk about the importance of what these guys modeled—that we're to seek Jesus in our lives.

3. Students can enter into this story by identifying with different characters. Discuss why each group of people was there that day. The people in the crowd were observers of the scene. The Pharisees and teachers were skeptical of who Jesus was, while the man lying before Jesus was in need of healing. The men on the roof would do anything, including tearing up a roof, to get their friend to Jesus.

4. Have your students note that the Bible says Jesus noticed the faith of the sick man and his friends (verse 20). As they look over the list and your selections, imagine God is answering this question for you. What would he think you need? Would he have different answers than your kids'?

CLOSE

Find a stretcher or sturdy cot and bring it out for an illustration. Have four students hold the four corners, and have another person come up and lie down on it. As the students carry the person around, have your group talk about what they notice. What do the carriers have to do to get their friend somewhere? How is this similar to what we need to do to help *our* friends get to Jesus? Have students look up Galatians 6:1-6 and discuss ways your group can help each other.

MORE

• **Discuss with your students how the actions of the friends showed their faith in Jesus. When does someone show their faith that a chair can hold them—when they think about the chair, or when they sit down on it? Explore the connection between faith and action and read James 2:14-20. Students can also look at these passages in Luke for more on faith: Luke 7:9; 8:48-50; 17:19; and 18:42.**

• **It may be that your students want to discuss how miracles can happen, or they may have friends who ask how miracles can happen. Don't run away from the opportunity to talk about this, but you'll want to do some reading so you can be prepared for the various questions. Two helpful books are *The Case for Christ* by Lee Strobel (Zondervan) and *Know Why You Believe* by Paul Little (InterVarsity Press).**

1. **In each pair, circle the word or phrase that best describes you when you have a bad cold or flu. I like to:**

> Be by myself (or) complain to others.
> Sleep a lot (or) watch TV.
>
> Eat chicken noodle soup (or) take medicine.
> Skip school (or) keep pushing on.
>
> Feel like the world is going to end (or) be optimistic that I'll feel better tomorrow.

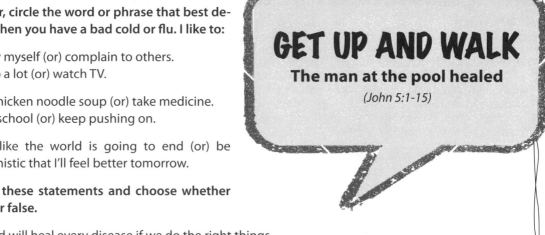

GET UP AND WALK
The man at the pool healed
(John 5:1-15)

2. **Check out these statements and choose whether they're true or false.**

> a. God will heal every disease if we do the right things. _____
>
> b. If a person isn't healed, it's because she doesn't have enough faith. _____
>
> c. No one is healed anymore—that was just for Bible times. _____
>
> d. God can heal every situation if he chooses to do so. _____

3. **Read John 5:1-8. Why do you think Jesus asks a man who had been crippled for 38 years if he wants to get well? Check one.**

> _____ He might be used to his condition and not want to change.
>
> _____ He wouldn't be able to beg anymore and would have to go to work.
>
> _____ Jesus was getting the man's attention so he knew what Jesus could do for him.
>
> _____ It was a test to see if the man had faith or not.

4. **Look up Mark 3:1-5 and read it. What was the main concern of the religious leaders?**

What did they want to do as a result?

5. **Jesus found the man in the temple (verses 14, 15) and reminded him to stop sinning or else something worse might happen. What's a possible explanation for what this means?**

> _____ The man was ungrateful and didn't obey God after he was healed.
>
> _____ The man would become crippled again if he didn't change.
>
> _____ Jesus was reminding him that the judgments of God were worse than being crippled.
>
> _____ The man was self-centered and wasn't truly grateful for his new life.

15. GET UP AND WALK—The man at the pool healed *(John 5:1-15)*

THIS WEEK

Your students live in a culture where personal health, happiness, and safety are some of the highest goals. Yet people still get sick and injured, and experience intense sorrow. Jesus healed others, a demonstration of his power, as God, over sickness and disease. One man who experienced Jesus' touch had sat crippled by the pool of Bethesda for a long time, part of a larger group of sick and crippled people. This TalkSheet connects his story to your students' lives as they recall their own injuries and illnesses and how Christ can yet make them whole—-spiritually, emotionally, and physically.

OPENER

On a whiteboard, write the following injuries or illnesses:

Scratched eye	Broken leg
A concussion (or being knocked out)	Chicken pox
Flu and fever	Broken ribs
Boils	Burning your hand
Sprained ankle	Pinkeye

Ask students to help you decide which of these (or others they can add) are the most painful. The most annoying? Ask students to imagine they've had one of the conditions listed on the board, and the effects of it had lasted for a year—and Jesus comes to them and heals them. What would that be like? What would you be feeling?

Transition by asking if anyone used to think—when they were younger—Band-Aids® had special healing abilities. Pass out a Band-Aid® to each person in the group. Have them put it on to remind them of the fact that we do get sick or injured. You'll use this visual aid later.

DISCUSSION

1. This question should get students reflecting on how they respond to being sick. They can begin to identify with the man in this story. After students share their questions, reread the story in John 5:1-15. This would be a great one to have four students act out as you read. Bring a small blanket for the mat and have two people serve as the Jewish leaders. You can either have the actors repeat the quotes (easiest) or have them memorize them beforehand. Ask students what they observed in the scene as it was depicted.
2. These statements reveal what your middle schoolers think about God's power and control. Walk through each of the first three while telling students how it limits God's power. Some may need to discuss the one about miracles for today if students have questions. The last one is correct because God is all-knowing and all-powerful and capable of healing as he desires.
3. Which ones did your students check? Let students discuss why they chose the one they did. The question seems to have been asked to bring the man's attention to what was about to happen—but all four could be possible reasons.
4. The command to observe a Sabbath day each week is a strong one in the Old Testament (Exodus 20:8-11). In fact, to disobey the Sabbath was punishable by death (Numbers 15:32-36) and blessings were promised for observing it (Isaiah 58:13). Originally intended for people's refreshment, the Sabbath was weighted down by the religious leaders' list of dos and don'ts. But Jesus confronted this list, as he had the right to do as Creator. After Pentecost the church gathered on the first day of the week to worship, pray, and financially support the work of the church (Acts 20:7; 1 Corinthians 16:2; Revelation 1:10).
5. All but the second choice are possible answers. Poll the students quickly on how many selected each statement to get your group's consensus. The first statement will likely be the most popular, so make sure to discuss the latter options. Which have any potential of being the best answer? Why or why not? Note that the man's answer to Jesus' question in verse 7 showed he still didn't get who was speaking to him, so this could be Jesus' reminder for this guy—that God had done the work so he'd better obey him!

CLOSE

Have students think about the Band-Aid® they put on. It serves as a reminder that we get sick and injured, experience difficulties, and go through ups and downs. Challenge your students: God never said he'd take those things completely out of our lives, but that he would help us get through them. Some of your kids (or their family members) have been through tough physical problems. You may want to allow them a minute to share how they're dealing with those. Close by saying that it's easy to think God has abandoned us when things don't go our way, but often that's when we can best show our reliance on God. Remind your kids that God can still heal people today. Read James 5:14-16 and, before closing with prayer, make sure to pray for any physical issues your students may be dealing with. You can have students remove their Band-Aids® as a reminder that someday there won't be any more sickness or pain.

MORE

• **One interesting theme in the book of John is the role water plays in describing God's work. The wedding at Cana changed common water used for washing dishes into the best wine, and Jesus told the woman at the well in Samaria that he was the living water who would satisfy her thirsty soul. Here a man has attempted to find healing in water, but only through Jesus can he experience what he needs. Explore this related idea of thirsts in our lives—desires for more—and how we can experience contentment. Read Ecclesiastes 5:10, Psalm 16, or Philippians 4:11-12 for more on contentment.**
• **If your students want to talk more about the Sabbath, Colossians 2:16 seems to suggest that there were various perspectives among Christians about what to do on that day. Christians no longer observed Jewish laws regarding the seventh day of the week, but gathered on the first day of the week for prayer, and still demonstrated a respect for the day ("the Lord's day" of Revelation 1:10). Some churches meet on Saturday. The issue isn't when, but what. Should Christians observe a day off each week? What does that look like? What should they do on that day?**

1. What is the most beautiful thing you've ever seen?

2. For each of these statements, put "T" next to ones that are true in your life and "F" next to any that are false in your life.

_____ I'm usually happy.

_____ I try to obey God.

_____ I'm fortunate or lucky.

_____ I care for others.

3. Get with two or three others and read verses 3-10 of Matthew 5. These verses show how those who are committed to God should act. As a group, select three of the verses, rewrite them in your own words and give an example of what it looks like for middle school students.

VERSE #	YOUR GROUP'S VERSION	WHAT DOES THIS LOOK LIKE?
i)		
ii)		
iii)		

4. By yourself, look over the three verses you just rewrote and described. To the right of each, give yourself a grade (A through F, with A being the highest) for how you've done at these over the past two weeks.

5. What are two steps you can take to raise your grade in one of these areas?

THIS WEEK

One of the most well-known parts of Jesus' ministry is the passage known as the Sermon on the Mount, which begins with a series of "blesseds" about what qualities a righteous person should have. In the previous chapter, Jesus said that the kingdom of heaven had come near (Matthew 4:17), so these are the kingdom values—quite a different list than what the Pharisees were teaching. This TalkSheet explores what it means to be beautiful to others according to Jesus' model for us.

OPENER

Light a candle in the room before students come in, but don't acknowledge it. Have the room well lighted so students don't focus on the candle. Read Zechariah 4:6—"'Not by might nor by power, but by my Spirit,' says the LORD Almighty." Make two columns on the whiteboard. Title the left column "Our Own Might and Power" and the right one "By God's Spirit." Ask students to describe them, and list their answers in the correct column. Ask your students the focus of each column. Is it possible to make a difference by acting with "might and power?" How? Transition into the discussion.

DISCUSSION

1. Write the word *beauty* on the board and ask students to construct a definition for it. After a bit, push students to think widely about it by asking if beauty is skin deep. Can there be beauty inside people? Can people reflect God's beauty?

2. These verses are called the Beatitudes, which comes from a Latin word that also means "blessed." In English, one is fortunate or happy when acting out values that show who God is. Discuss what it means to be happy. What makes your students happy? Is happiness present only when things go their way? Does it come and go? Is it different from being joyful?

3. This will take some time, but it is the main focus of this TalkSheet. On the left side of the board, write the numbers 3 through 10 in a column. Have students say their rewritten versions. You can write the essence of each new version verse next to its number, or have students come up and do it. You may want to leave room on the right to be able to write what each looks like. If the groups avoided any verses, work on those as a large group, and feel free to explore why no one picked that verse. When the board is complete, ask students what would happen if people started to act like this. How would that be beautiful? Which one would be the most difficult?

4. The goal for right behavior isn't to appear good or to try to display our spirituality to others. The goal should be to reflect Jesus through how we live—to show people through our kindness, helpfulness, and love that Christ is the center of our lives.

5. What would happen if everyone in your group decided to work at reflecting Jesus' love toward others, and to one another? What would that look like? How could they support each other in such a process?

CLOSE

Read Matthew 5:14-16 and point out that, just as Jesus said he is *the* light (John 8:12), we are to be lights that reflect him. Ask students to come up with as many things that a light does as they can. If applicable, connect some of the Beatitudes to students' answers, showing them how they're light-giving to others. Remind students that their job is to make sure the light shines. Draw everyone's attention to the candle that's been burning the whole time. What does it mean to "let your light shine" before others? Tell students that sometimes they have opportunities to be light when others are experiencing darkness. Turn off the lights in the room. Invite students to look at the light for about a minute. Ask students what they notice. It's the same light, but what's different? Close by discussing with students what it means to let your light shine, and how the Beatitudes make it beautiful and reflect more of God's light in the world. You may want to close by reading verses 3-12 from *The Message*. You can close with prayer that your kids will let their lights shine as they reflect more of God.

MORE

• **You may want to set-up a "random acts of kindness" event for a weekend. Your group can choose a variety of helpful activities to do in their community—without expectation of a donation. Some groups pass out new water bottles to customers leaving a local department store. Others do work for needy people in the local church, and a simple one is a free car wash that's actually free.**

• **There are some popular songs that talk about beauty that could spark discussion on how people describe and view beauty. They may not all be appropriate, so preview them. "Beautiful" is a popular song title, no matter the genre, including Christian music. Google "beautiful lyrics" and look for various songs to find an appropriate stanza about beauty to discuss with your students. What does each verse say about beauty? Who decides what's beautiful? Brainstorm ways that we can reflect God's beauty to others.**

1. **Rank the following on how important they are to your relationship with God. Use a scale of 1 (lowest) to 10 (highest).**

Prayer _____   Reading the Bible _____

Going to church _____   Summer camp _____

Retreats _____   Going to youth group _____

Friends _____   Parents _____

Christian adults _____   Christian books _____

Music _____   Television _____

2. **People give money for a variety of reasons. Why have you given money? Check all that apply.**

___ For someone's birthday.

___ To support missions.

___ To a relative in need.

___ To obey God.

___ Tithe or offering at church.

___ In secret—to help someone else.

___ So God will bless with more.

___ To support a good cause.

3. **Complete the following sentence: "In the last week, I prayed _____ times other than at a meal."**

The three most common things I prayed for are:

1.

2.

3.

Look over the Lord's Prayer in Matthew 6:9-13. What did Jesus pray about?

4. **Define what it means to "fast".**

Have you ever gone without something important for a while—on purpose? List it below and explain what happened:

5. **Read Psalm 25:4-7 and rewrite it in your own words as if it were your prayer:**

THIS WEEK

It's easy to see being a Christian as the way we act, a bunch of dos and don'ts we're supposed to follow. Faithfulness is important, yes, but there were moments when Jesus focused on the reasons and spirit behind our actions. Many religious people appeared to be spiritual, but lacked a right motivation and even faith. This TalkSheet exposes students to some of the important spiritual practices and what Jesus says about them.

OPENER

Scripture skits. Think through some skit ideas ahead of time in case any groups get stuck. Divide the students into four groups, giving a section of this chapter to each group. Give each group a title and a passage on an index card: Helping the poor—Matthew 6:1-4; Prayer—Matthew 6:5-8; Fasting—Matthew 6:16-18; and Money—Matthew 6:19-24. Have them come up with a live skit (or YouTube video, if that helps) that illustrates the passage in a fun way. They need to have a narrator who will read the passage while the others act out a two-minute skit. Give them five to seven minutes to work on ideas and then have them perform their skits. After you've finished watching the performances, ask students for any responses they may have. Write the four areas on the board (helping the poor, prayer, fasting, and money) and ask students to share reasons why spiritual people should care about them.

DISCUSSION

1. You can discuss this one in various ways. Which items were highest for everyone? Lowest? You can have a few people share their rankings for each one. Or someone can find the average for your group (it may take awhile). Finish by summarizing your observations—do students agree that they're accurate?

2. Do people give money for all these reasons? Which reasons are the best? Read Matthew 6:2-3. What is Jesus saying about how we should give? What was happening that Jesus was trying to confront? What reward were the boasting givers seeking? What reward should we be seeking when we give?

3. Ask students to look quietly over their answers. If they were to write a prescription to help their prayer life, what would it be? Tell students to write their prescription along the right side of their paper. Ask them to include two action steps.

4. Fasting isn't eating physical food and replacing it with spiritual food. It's more than just skipping a meal—it's adding in a time of spiritual discipline such as Bible reading or prayer to provide spiritual nourishment. Can we fast from something other than food? What about a media fast? Or fast from a certain food (such as soda, chocolate, pizza, or beets) for a longer period?

5. What happens when we lose sight of what Jesus sees as spiritual? How do people mess up what God intended? What happens that causes us to get self-centered in our reasons for going to church, praying, reading the Bible, or "doing" our Christian walk?

CLOSE

Encourage students to recommit themselves to fostering their spiritual lives, even in the middle of schedules and lives that work against it. Challenge students to be tough on themselves as they think about the things they do just so others see them as being "good Christians." Close by leading your group in the Lord's Prayer.

MORE

• What defines a person as a Christian is an important topic for middle schoolers as most of them operate with either a transaction-based (I made a decision) or performance-based (what I do makes me good or bad) definition. Being a Christian is more than a one-time decision based on what we do—it's an ongoing relationship with (John 15:4) and faith in Jesus Christ that produces right actions. You may want to have students examine what the apostle Paul thought. Read 2 Corinthians 11:16-30, Galatians 6:14-15, and 1 Timothy 1:15-16. Have students list how Paul defined what it meant for him to be a Christian. How does that list compare to how most Christians today define themselves?

• What are other ways that friends of your middle schoolers try to act spiritual? Does anyone have friends who believe in astrology? Mess with Ouija boards? Explore this with your students. Most research shows teens are more traditional in their religious beliefs than we think. It may be appropriate to discuss spiritual practices and look at the Lord's Prayer, not as a model for just how to pray, but as a way to focus on God and his kingdom as the truth.

1. When you think of the phrase "treasures of Egypt," what images come to mind?

What other great treasures are there in the world?

2. Which of these will last the longest? Write down how many years each of the following will probably last.

____ Your favorite video game system   ____ Where you live

____ Your athletic or physical abilities   ____ Your prayers

____ Your acts of kindness to others   ____ Your example to friends

____ A car   ____ Your relationship with God

3. What do you value most? Write down the most important stuff for each of these areas:

Your reputation -

What you own -

Your relationship with God -

How you look -

How you spend your free time -

4. Read Hebrews 11:24-26 and write down everything Moses chose.

What did Moses avoid or give up?

5. Read what Jesus said in Matthew 6:19-21. Where did he say your heart would be?

Write down three or four areas of your life that can reveal where your treasure is.

THIS WEEK

Though they don't have jobs, middle schoolers still experience the effects of a culture that teaches that the goal of life is to make yourself happy by getting new and better stuff. One chief topic in Jesus' ministry was money, an area that reveals our true desires. Using this as a starting point, this TalkSheet focuses on the word *treasure* and lets middle schoolers discover and discuss the real treasure they're to seek—God's kingdom.

OPENER

When they were little, did your students have a toy or an object that they named? Maybe they named a blanket, bike, sports item, or stuffed animal. Get as many examples as students want to offer. Be sensitive and don't allow teasing. Do any of your students' families have a name for their car or van? Why do people give names to objects? Discuss what it means when we give names to objects. Let your middle schoolers know that Jesus taught a *lot* about money. In fact, Jesus said it could control us so much that he gave it a name—*Mammon*—which his listeners would have known as the Money God. More than money, it included the property and wealth—our stuff—that control what we value, think, and do. How could love for our stuff motivate us to act very differently from what God wants?

DISCUSSION

1. Ancient Egyptian civilization did an amazing job of preserving its great treasures for thousands of years. Your students should be able to remember King Tut, the pyramids, and the mummies. Discuss with students what other great treasures exist. Did your students have any treasures they kept hidden when they were younger?

2. We sometimes put our happiness in items that are fragile and very temporary. Discuss with students whether they ever feel satisfied with what they have. Can anyone remember a toy they really wanted that didn't last very long once they got it? Talk through students' answers to this one. Did they consider that their prayers might last for a long time (see the symbolism in Revelation 8:4)? How can our example to ...last for a long time?

... ...ddle schoolers value in each of these ar-

eas? Ask your students what they wrote. Don't make this question legalistic and leave students feeling like they aren't doing enough. It's important to play and rest—both are gifts of God. Your focus for discussing this question is mostly on what, not how much.

4. So why did Moses give up his claim to some of the treasures of Egypt? What might the results have been in choosing sin over following Christ? Is it difficult today to seek God and his values over the world?

5. What do we feel when we're seeking something we treasure? Have students think about sports teams or events, musical groups, or television shows. What about where we spend our money? Time? What we think about? Are there other indicators your students noted?

CLOSE

Tell students how Jesus concluded this section by reading Matthew 6:33: "But seek first his kingdom and his righteousness, and all these things will be given to you as well." Write on the board, "A kingdom is wherever the desires and power of the king are being realized." Ask students: If we're to seek God's kingdom first, what should we be doing? What does it mean to seek God's righteousness? Challenge students that this is where they should be investing their treasure. It doesn't mean we then get the stuff we want, but it does mean Jesus can satisfy the deepest desires of our heart (Psalm 37:4; Matthew 19:29).

MORE

• There are some good scenes from the *National Treasure* movies you can use. You can show the trailer for the movie, or cue either movie to the scene where the main characters are about to discover the treasure room. Play the scene to show the reactions of the characters when they realized what they'd found. Discuss the treasure and the goal for those who sought it. What do you do once you have a treasure?

• To dig in a bit more on treasure, have students check out Matthew 2:9-11; 12:35; 13:34; 19:16-22; 1 Timothy 6:6-10; 17-19; and James 5:2, 3. What does each of these say about treasure? What together do they teach us that we're to do with our treasure?

Thanks to Rob Wegner of Granger Community Church (www.gc-cwired.com) for some of the ideas in this session.

1. When you were little, what were you scared of? Write down fears of monsters, the dark, food, or other issues you can remember:

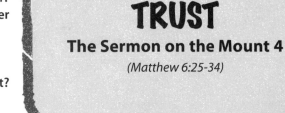

TRUST

The Sermon on the Mount 4

(Matthew 6:25-34)

Over the past week, what have you worried about? Write as many worries as you can remember.

2. Read Matthew 6:25-34 and answer the following:

How much would a sparrow cost at a local pet store? _____

How many shirts do you own? _____

Do you worry more about clothes, food, or your body? _____

What's your favorite flower? _____

3. Jesus points out three problems. Read each verse and identify the problem with worry.

Verse 27:

Verse 30:

Verse 32:

Verse 34:

4. Verse 33 says to "Seek first his kingdom and his righteousness, and all these things will be given to you as well." Give some examples of what putting God first looks like.

5. Get with two or three others, read the end of the Sermon on the Mount (Matthew 7:24-27), and answer these questions:

What are two possible ways that people could respond to Jesus' message?

Describe what Jesus says is the wise option:

What happens to those who are wise?

THIS WEEK

The Sermon on the Mount ends with a gentle invitation from Jesus for his listeners to trust in God. It can be difficult to do, because we get to do whatever we want and make our own choices. Middle schoolers are still discovering who God is at a time where anxiousness and worry can often be serious obstacles to trust. This relevant TalkSheet explores this powerful passage and connects it to the core issue for middle schoolers—who they're going to trust.

OPENER

Tell students you're going to make the floor into a "worry scale." Those who worry a lot can move to the right of the room. Those who never worry should move toward the left wall. Those who say they're in the middle, which shouldn't be many, can stand in the middle of the room. The rest can stand wherever they are on the worry line, somewhere between the right and left walls. Tell students to be prepared to explain their choices for the spots they chose for themselves on the scale. Play some instrumental music and start them working on this. After five minutes, stop the music and have a fast-paced discussion—you want to hear why students place themselves where they are on the worry scale.

DISCUSSION

1. To get students talking out loud, ask them to share any funny or unusual fears they remember from childhood. Anxiety seems more common at this age, and teenagers seem to suffer most, or at least most readily show the symptoms. Tell students that while anxiety and worry are common in middle school, they aren't healthy in large doses. Point out their list of worries from the past week. Ask for a show of hands: How many had more than three? Is it possible not to worry? Shouldn't we worry about something? Isn't it impossible *not* to be anxious? Is anxiousness okay, or is it a sign of a serious problem?

2. Find out what a sparrow costs. Discuss the answers with your students. Ask students what they do when they're anxious. Are any of them pacers who like to walk around? Do any bite their fingernails? Do any lose sleep when they're uptight about stuff? Do some get angry or hide from the problem? Do any students pursue habits such as video games or sleep to try to numb the anxiety?

3. Let students share what they wrote while you write

highlights from their answers on the board. No one can add anything to their life by worrying—not time (verse 27) or lack of trouble (verse 32). The issue with worry is a lack of trust in God (verse 30), and that worry reflects values that aren't from God (verse 32). That's strong stuff! So what can they do?

4. The answer is to put God and his kingdom first. What does that look like? Help students process basic steps they can take to put God first.

5. Is it possible to build partially or occasionally on a solid foundation? Have students describe what they think of when they think of a wise person. What does wisdom look like? Why is it wise to trust God for your future?

CLOSE

Have students close their eyes and reflect on their level of fear, worry, and mistrust. Remind them of some areas as they reflect—family, work, school, sports, friends, dating life, future, and so on. After a minute, tell students to imagine Jesus sitting down with them and talking about these matters. What would he say? What would that scene be like? What would the setting be? The tone of voice? The nonverbal expressions? Would your students feel more able to trust him and not worry about stuff?

MORE

• **Before the meeting, set a series of signs or images around the room that represent some of the chief concerns in life: Good job, healthy family, good diet, trendy clothes, following God's will, money, fun vacations, and so on. Don't have more than 10 stations from which they can choose. In front of each sign, put a bowl or box. Divide the students into equal groups of no more than eight people. Give each group play money of equal amounts ($100 would work well). Tell students they're to spend their play money on what's important to their group. They'll need to establish the worth of different areas so they can spend their total. They may decide that a good job is worth $30, so they put $30 of the play money in that box. Once completed, have someone go around and total what was spent on each area.**
• **Worry can be a symptom of a larger issue in life, like a poor parent/child relationship or an inability to trust others or God. This passage reassures us that the Father feeds us (verse 26), the Father clothes us (verse 30), and the Father knows us (verse 32). You can use other passages (Matthew 6:8; Philippians 4:6; and 1 Peter 5:7) to discuss anxiety and worry with your students.**

1. Circle one of the following that you think best describes what sin is.

Missing the mark

Rebelling against God

Twisting what God intended

> # FORGIVENESS AT THE MASTER'S FEET
> ### The Pharisee and the woman anointing Jesus
> *(Luke 7:36-50)*

2. Read Luke 7:36-50. Describe each of the other two people in the story besides Jesus.

Simon the Pharisee

The repentant woman

3. Read Luke 7:16 and then look again at verse 39. Why do you think the Pharisee invited Jesus to his house? Check one.

_____ He was curious about who Jesus was.

_____ He was trying to check out whether Jesus was a prophet.

_____ He was just being polite to a guest in his town.

_____ It was the right thing to do and he wanted to look good to others.

4. Write down two times where you wronged someone (a parent, friend, coach, or teacher) and got in big trouble. For each one, describe how you received forgiveness.

TROUBLE TIME   HOW WERE YOU FORGIVEN?

5. In verse 47, Jesus explains why the woman displayed such love toward him. How do you show love to God? Write down as many ways that you can remember when you've shown your love to God.

THIS WEEK

This session is a vivid illustration of God's compassion, love, and forgiveness for those who put their faith in Jesus Christ. This TalkSheet helps students develop their understanding of sin, a prominent biblical theme, and how God extends forgiveness to those who respond to the gospel message.

OPENER

What sin is the "worst"? Have students discuss this with you and see if they can "rank" sins. Ask students for a list of 15 to 20 sins and write them on the board. Have students divide them into three groups by telling you which society considers the worst, which are in between, and which are considered not such a big deal. Some students point out that all sins are equal since they're all disobedience to God. Help students think about this by asking whether some actions (such as murder or sexual sin) involve more than one sin. Challenge students to include the foundational sins of pride, envy, and jealousy. Where would they rank? Do they lead to any of the other sins? Can God forgive all of these? Read a story of forgiveness in which Jesus forgives the debt of a woman in the presence of a proud religious person (Luke 7:36-50).

DISCUSSION

1. All three are biblical descriptions for sin. Have a verse or two ready for each to read. Missing the mark— Hosea 13:2; Romans 6:12; and James 1:15. Rebelling against God—Exodus 23:33; 1 Kings 8:50; and Matthew 7:23. Twisting what God intended—Psalm 51:4; Daniel 9:5; and Romans 8:7.

2. Tell students to include in their descriptions aspects like motivation, social standing, and other less obvious characteristics. When they're finished, have students share what they wrote. Ask students which of the two was a sinner. The answer is both—Simon was proud and unaware of his own sin (Luke 18:9-14, for example), and we're all sinners (Romans 3:23). The woman was well aware of her sins, which were forgiven because of her faith in Christ. It's important to let students know God doesn't hate sinners—instead, he offers forgiveness.

3. Simon the Pharisee was seen as an important person, and an invitation for Jesus to eat in his home was a significant event in that neighborhood. Uninvited people could come too, but they would have to stand in the background to merely watch and listen. The woman broke many social customs with her sinful life, her exposed hair, and her use of her hair to wipe the dirt away from Jesus' feet. How does this show her faith in Christ?

4. Ask your students what it feels like to be forgiven. It's so difficult to truly forgive. Those who have been forgiven—how did it feel after that? Was there a sense of peace, that everything was okay? Why did you have that feeling of peace that everything would be okay?

5. Remind students that the penalty for sin is death (Romans 6:23), but the gift of God is eternal life through his Son and our decision to put our faith in him and follow him (Romans 10:9-10). Challenge students that their relationship with God is a relationship with a *living* God, one who wants us to be close and express our love to him.

CLOSE

This story provides a great opportunity to examine our own lives and respond to Jesus and his Spirit. Have students look over their answers to the last question and tell them you're going to give them an opportunity to respond to God today. You can either lead them in a prayer of confession or you can pass out 3 x 5 cards and have them write a prayer to God. Offer students who want to commit their lives to Christ the opportunity to meet in another room. Whatever your tradition, close by allowing an opportunity for students to pray for forgiveness, to experience Christ's love for the first time, or to consider their own response to God's leading in their lives.

MORE

• **The woman's actions were dramatic as she expressed her love for Jesus. Is it difficult for you to demonstrate your love for God? Is it easier in private or in public? In what ways do people demonstrate that today? How did the woman know her sins were forgiven? How do we know our sins are forgiven? (Acts 13:38-39; 1 John 1:9; and Hebrews 8:12.)**

• **Galatians 5:6 says, "The only thing that counts is faith expressing itself through love." Is it faith, or is it love that saves people from their sins (Ephesians 2:8-9)? How does "faith expressing itself through love" look in each of our lives? In our youth group? How can we as a group show our love for God?**

1. For each of the following, rate yourself on a scale of 1 to 10, with 10 being "a lot like me" and 1 being "not like me at all."

_____ I keep my promises.

_____ I talk the same way everyone else does at my school.

_____ I talk differently at school than I do at church.

_____ The words I use change depending on which friends I'm around.

_____ I've used some words even though I didn't know what they meant.

_____ I like to sound like I know what I'm talking about.

_____ I can easily say "I'm sorry" and admit I'm wrong.

BE CAREFUL WHAT YOU SAY
Jesus warns the Pharisees
(Matthew 12:35-37)

2. Which best describes the thought process you use to decide how you speak?

❏ Thought process? What's that?
❏ I just go with the flow, like everyone else.
❏ Every day is a creative opportunity.
❏ I speak only what others need to know.
❏ I try not to talk that much.
❏ I'm very careful not to say anything bad.

3. Check out Matthew 12:22-24. What did the Pharisees say about Jesus?

Now read verses 35-37. What warning did Jesus give?

4. Rewrite the following verses in your own words.

Psalm 19:14—

2 Timothy 2:14—

5. What we say is important in that it can help others *and* ourselves. Sometimes we need to share honestly, and that's difficult to do! How easy or difficult is it for you to share your deepest feelings with each of these people?

Your close friends—

Your parents—

Your youth group leaders—

God—

THIS WEEK

Our words tell a lot about what's important to us. It doesn't take much time watching television to realize that what we laugh at and choose to quote isn't always the most God-honoring stuff. That can carry over into our conversations, and before we know it, we're talking in ways that may not reflect what God desires. This TalkSheet allows your middle schoolers to discuss what they say in light of Jesus' teaching and to realize that what they say can be a blessing to others.

OPENER

Ask students which TV show or movie they quote the most. Does their everyday conversation feature certain quotes from movies or TV shows?

What comes to your students' minds when they think of "empty words"? Develop a definition and write it on the board. What idle words or empty words do they hear people use? Are slang words considered empty? What about "Christian cussing"—words that sound close to what people consider swearing? Are they careless or idle words (Ephesians 5:4)? What about sarcastic comments? Promises they don't keep? Promises to God they don't follow? What about telling someone you love them when you mean something else? Close this section by summarizing how their spoken words have a tremendous effect on others and reveal a lot about ourselves.

DISCUSSION

1. Let students share a bit about what they noticed from their rankings. Were any difficult to decide? Is it difficult for your students to be careful of what they say? Make sure your students can share honestly without fear of being ridiculed or thought of as different.
2. Get some quick responses here. Have students raise their hands to indicate their answers.
3. The Pharisees were growing more concerned about Jesus and his teachings, and they tried to explain where Jesus got his power. In the same way, what are things people say about God that aren't true?
4. What did your students come up with on their rewrites? What are the principles in each of these verses? What would happen if you put these principles into practice? Is it even a big deal to be careful of what we say?

5. Get students talking about what role words play in their lives. Have they ever sent a text message or email message that was misunderstood? Why did the misunderstanding happen? Many times, it's because there wasn't any nonverbal communication. What makes it difficult to talk about how we feel with others? Why is it easier to communicate in writing (letters, text, IM, email) than face to face? What makes talking more "real"?

CLOSE

The principle today is that words have power. While we can be careless with words, words can also have significant positive impact. In Scripture, there are many examples of a spoken blessing having great significance. The New Testament contains examples of spoken benedictions—a blessing to an audience as they're dismissed. Close by reading one passage (Romans 5:5-6, 13, and 33 or Hebrews 13:20-21) and then praying for your students that their words this week would reflect the meditation of their hearts.

MORE

• **Before the meeting, find 10 "in" words or phrases you and your friends used when you were the age of your students, and words commonly used before your time. List them on a sheet of paper with room for students to write in the meaning after each one. For help, check out www.onlineslangdictionary.com and www.alpha-dictionary.com/slang for usable words. Be discerning and appropriate. When the meeting starts, help your students discover how words change by having a slang competition. Ask students to name some of the (appropriate) "in" phrases they hear at school. List these phrases with their meanings on the whiteboard. Then give them a quiz of "cool" words that were commonly used by the generations before them.**
• **For some further Bible study on words and what we say, check out Deuteronomy 23:21-23; Numbers 30:1-4 on vows; Isaiah 57:3-4; Psalm 89:34; and Proverbs 17:27-28. What do these verses say about our speech? So many times people focus on words by pointing out what *not* to say. What are some things we *should* say to others in our lives?**

1. How helpful are you? Rate yourself below.

← • →

I love to help
and it's easy to do so.

It's hard for me
to help others.

2. Describe a time when you were helpful to some group of people.

GOOD DEEDS FROM AN UNLIKELY SOURCE
The Good Samaritan
(Luke 10:25-37)

3. Read Luke 10:25-37. The expert answered Jesus by saying the Samaritan was the one who showed mercy. Read each of the following and write what it says about mercy.

Proverbs 11:17—

Zechariah 7:9—

Romans 12:5—

4. If you helped in each situation, which of the following would show the greatest amount of mercy?

__ A woman spills a bag of groceries in the parking lot and they roll all over.

__ Your church bulletin asks for volunteers to help landscape all day on a Saturday.

__ A new kid at your school regularly sits by himself or herself in the cafeteria.

__ Outside your local Wal-Mart, a guy holds a "will work for food" sign.

__ Your parent asks you to do the dishes and clean up the kitchen.

__ The neighbor's kids are always coming over to see what you're doing.

5. Read Galatians 6:10. What does "as we have opportunity" mean?

THIS WEEK

The Good Samaritan is often one of the first Bible stories children learn in church, but for Jesus' listeners it was an unthinkable possibility—a Samaritan helping a Jewish man left for dead by his own people. This TalkSheet takes a familiar story that Jesus told and challenges middle schoolers to think about their own willingness to help others around them.

OPENER

Tell students you're going to check on how helpful they are with a Good Samaritan Quiz. Each scenario has three options. Students are to move to the part of the room that represents the option they choose. Have students stand, then read each option so students can move to the designated spots. Feel free to make observations about your group's choices. Be appropriate and affirming.

• Your mom reminds you to clean your room. Do you do it right away, put it off until later that day, or argue that it's clean enough already?

• Someone's books and papers fall all over the hallway at school. Do you laugh, immediately help pick them up, or feel good because you're the one who knocked them out of the person's hands?

• When there's an obvious job to be done around the house, are you reluctant to help, usually waiting to be asked, or quick to do it before your parents have to?

• If you saw a guy in the Wal-Mart parking lot asking for some money for gas, would you give it to him, ignore him, or be mad that he's bugging you?

• When your church or school has a service day in your town, do you make sure you can show up to help, see if it fits your schedule, or assume others will cover it?

Inform students that it's easy to *read* about being helpful or to serve while on a youth group event, but it's another thing to do it in our everyday lives.

DISCUSSION

1. Let students share how they determined where to put themselves on this scale. What were the determining factors that pushed them to either end of the scale?

2. Let students share their stories. What kind of helping moments did they share? What are some of the barriers that keep them from helping others? In the story of the Good Samaritan, what were the reasons the first guys didn't help? The two men in the story avoided the man because he would've made them ceremonially unclean—even though they had the time and opportunity to help. What excuses do people use today?

3. The Bible is full of reminders and stories of the mercy God shows us, so we should be merciful to others. Jesus tells this story as an answer to a trick question someone asked him. How does his response show mercy?

4. There really isn't a right answer for this one. In fact, you may want to ask if there are greater amounts of mercy or not. Were any of these situations not really about showing mercy? Allow students to share their opinions and reasons.

5. Make a list on the board of the kinds of opportunities your students get to be helpful. Do opportunities happen by themselves or do we have to make them happen?

CLOSE

The expert asked Jesus how someone could have eternal life. After Jesus asked what the Scripture said, the teacher quoted Deuteronomy 6:5 and Leviticus 19:18—that we're to love God with our whole hearts and to love others as much as we love ourselves.

Point out to students that the first step is to truly love God. How do we love God? In what ways can we work on loving him with our whole heart? The second part is to love others as much as we love ourselves. What does "as much as ourselves" imply? You may want to discuss how self-centeredness keeps people from being loving to each other.

MORE

• **For more on helpfulness, have students read any of the following: Acts 20:36; 1 Thessalonians 5:14; 1 Timothy 6:2; Titus 3:5. The command to love the "Lord your God" comes from Deuteronomy 6:5, whereas the command to love one another comes from Leviticus 19:18.**

• **Find episodes of basic helpful issues on cartoons like *SpongeBob SquarePants* or any old television shows you remember. The Veggie Tales series has an episode titled "Are You My Neighbor?" about this story. As always, prescreen the videos and find a four- to five-minute scene that would work as a good kickoff to the TalkSheet discussion.**

• **Preview a great YouTube.com video that may challenge your students and serve well before the opener: www.youtube.com/watch?v=IcK2iaT3TkU.**

1. For each pair of phrases below, put a checkmark next to the one that gets the most attention on how it looks for you and your family:

_____Front yard / Back yard _____

_____Outside of car / Inside of car _____

_____ Family room / Bedroom _____

_____Clothes / Physical health _____

_____Actions at school / Actions at home _____

_____My reputation / My character _____

_____Activities at church / My devotions _____

LOOKING GOOD ON THE OUTSIDE
The six woes
(Luke 11:39-52)

2. Come up with a definition for what a hypocrite is.

3. Based on your definition, who of the following would you say is a hypocrite?

Juan attends church each week and would say he's a committed Christian. He occasionally reads his Bible, but has difficulty controlling his mouth, especially when he's around his friends. He's working on it, and prays about it, but it has been a problem for him.

Lori goes to church and likes to see her friends there. She goes to all the youth group events, but doesn't really listen or care. She tells all her friends she's a Christian, but when she's away from her church friends, she acts very differently.

Emma is a respected student at school and participates in school activities. She's a leader in her youth group at church. At home, though, she's often irritable and angry. She and her parents are trying to address it, but it's been going on for a while.

Andy doesn't really go to church and hasn't really thought much about God. He regularly acts mean toward others and treats girls in ways that aren't God-honoring.

4. Jesus confronted some religious people who looked godly on the outside but were different on the inside. Look up Luke 11 and answer the following:

What did the Pharisees neglect (verse 42)?

What did they love (verse 43)?

What didn't the Pharisees want to do (verse 46)?

What did they do to those they teach (verse 52)?

5. Think of one area where your actions in private are different from what others see about you. Write down one step you can take to give that area to God so you can be more like Jesus in private and when others can see you.

THIS WEEK

A common excuse for why people don't go to church or believe in God is because the Christians they know are just a bunch of hypocrites—people who pretend to be Christian, but act very differently. This TalkSheet tackles that topic, shows what it meant to be a hypocrite in Jesus' day, and connects that to the consistency of students' faith steps.

OPENER

Have students share what's popular for middle school students to wear. What kind of hairstyles are in? Jeans (wide or narrow, brands)? Do any of your students have a style that's different from others? Are high schoolers dressing the same as or differently than middle schoolers? What was in style 10 years ago? Find some pictures on the Internet of styles from 10, 20, and 30 years ago and show a one- or two-minute slideshow of how styles have changed. Remind students that these were "in" then.

Transition by noting how we spend a lot of time trying to look good to others—and that may be very different from what we're like when no one's looking. Jesus confronted the Pharisees about their focus on religion while they didn't have any love for God or others. Talk about how that's important for us to remember, too—it would be dreadful if we looked like Christians on the outside, but on the inside our character wasn't like Christ's at all.

DISCUSSION

1. What do students notice about their choices? Do they lean toward the outward or external, or do they lean toward the inside or internal choices?

2. Write a group definition on the board by having students share what they wrote. Underneath write the words *reputation* and *character*. Ask which of these is the biggest concern to a hypocrite.

3. How did your students determine what hypocrisy is or isn't? Only Lori should be the hypocrite—someone who says he's something he isn't. Juan and Emma are working on their issues, while Andy isn't wearing a mask at all. How would the Pharisees treat these people? What would Jesus want us to do?

4. Read Luke 11:39-52 out loud. Let students know that "woe" means "how dreadful for you."
   a. Verse 42—The Pharisees were so strict in their religiosity they even tithed on herbs and spices—while not caring for those in need (Micah 6:7-8).
   b. Verse 43—They loved to impress others with their presence. Have any of your middle schoolers seen someone do that?
   c. Verse 46—They loaded people down with rules, but weren't willing to help others at all. Challenge students that this is easy for us to do—to have higher expectations for others than we have for ourselves. (For example, we can get angry, but we get ticked when others get angry. Or we want forgiveness when we mess up, but if someone else does, we don't forgive…or forget.
   d. Verse 52—They made following God difficult to understand instead of working to help others understand it clearly. So people weren't able to follow God and enter his kingdom.

5. Challenge students to get with a trusted Christian adult (you?) in the next two weeks to talk about the challenge of living clean on both the outside and inside. Let them know you're available, as are other youth group leaders, and that it's a safe conversation (you won't pile on heavy loads).

CLOSE

This TalkSheet should connect well to students' lives, so you can close any number of ways—be creative! Read Luke 11:39-40 and discuss how people can get "clean" through God's forgiveness and faith in Christ. Close by reading Psalm 51:10-12 and one of the following: Praying for your students' answers to question #5, singing a song like "As the Deer Pants for the Water," or having a written reflection time. Let students write on a slip of paper an area where they're acting one way on the outside and quite opposite from what God wants on the inside. (Play some reflective music during the writing time.) Have them come up to a large cup that's dirty on the inside, a symbol of recognition that this area isn't clean. Have the students tear it up as they offer it to God, place it in the dirty cup, and leave it behind when they go back to their seats.

MORE

• A week or more before this session, leave an inch (2.5 cm) of coffee in the bottom of a nice clean coffee cup and let it sit out. It will become tarry and moldy. As an object lesson, hold up the cup and ask if anyone would like to take a drink from the cup—but don't let students see the inside. Few will decide whether they want to drink without first looking inside. It's not the outside of a cup that matters, but the inside. Do Christians put too much emphasis on the outside? Doesn't the outside (our actions and words) reveal what's going on inside? What are the inside issues people need to work on?

• The Pharisees were debating whether, during ritual purification, one actually had to clean the inside of the cups. Jesus used this debate to teach a larger spiritual truth. In the other "woes," Jesus was highly critical when he said (verse 44) that the Pharisees were perpetually unclean (Numbers 19:16), as if they'd been around dead bodies. Because so many people were buried in unmarked graves, the graves were often whitewashed so people could avoid coming in contact with them. Is it possible for Christians to be so mean, so full of rules for others, or so hypocritical that they keep others from becoming Christians (verse 52)? What can your group do to help each other not let that happen?

1. At the time of Jesus' teaching, the smallest item people knew in everyday life was a mustard seed. Write down the two smallest items you know, one in each of the blanks in the following sentences:

Life is like a _____ because _____.

Life is like a _____ because _____.

Now complete each sentence above, giving an example of how life can be like that object.

2. In what area of your life have you seen the most growth: 1) Over the past two years? 2) Since you were a child? Write down as many examples of growth as you can remember:

3. Get with one or two others around you and read Mark 4:26-32. Jesus' main teaching topic was about the kingdom of God. Different from a political kingdom, this was, and is, a spiritual kingdom with Jesus at the center. Work with your group members to look up the following verses and write down what each says about the kingdom of God.

Mark 1:15—

Mark 10:14-16—

Romans 14:17—

4. Look through this list of ways that the kingdom of God grows. Put a check next to the three you want to do best.

___ Being a good example in following Christ.
___ Obeying what the Bible says.
___ Giving my time to help the poor or needy.
___ Standing up for others at school.
___ Praying that God uses me to help others.

___ Serving others without notice.
___ Sharing my faith through words.
___ Trying to reach my friends for Christ.
___ Being an advocate for children.
___ Growing a heart for missions to the world.

5. Look around the room and really notice the people around you. Imagine that, as you leave today, your entire group is being "planted" in the world to grow God's kingdom through your actions and words. Write down two specific things you can do this week to do just that.

THIS WEEK

From the very beginning of his teaching, Jesus spoke of the kingdom of God. This theological concept is important when thinking about what it means to be the church (or part of the church) within today's culture. Students need to understand that the kingdom of God is a present reality in which God's will and power are being expressed—and that affects how they should live out their faith each week. This session uses two parables to introduce students to what Jesus meant by the "kingdom of God" and apply it to their lives.

OPENER

Announce that you're going to play a rousing game of The Experts' Club, and you want to select three of your best exaggerators who can act like they know what they're talking about even when they have no clue! Look for volunteers, but select the three that will do the best job up front. Bring the three up front and tell the group that each person will have two minutes (no more!) to explain how a seed grows. The group should vote on who did the best job at seeming expert and give that person a fabulous prize (it's best if it's a bag of candy they can share with everyone).

Then transition into the session by letting them know that no one knows how a seed knows to grow—it just does. In the same way, Jesus taught that the kingdom of God is like a tiny seed that, when it's planted, grows into a very large plant. Tell students that the kingdom of God was an important subject in Jesus' teaching.

DISCUSSION

1. Your students will be having fun after the opening, and you'll want to keep that rolling. After a few minutes, ask if anyone has one that's funny. Allow sharing from whoever wants to. If time permits, quickly ask if anyone has one to share that is especially insightful. Make sure you don't have the same students sharing on this second one.

2. People experience growth in multiple ways—physically, socially, mentally, and spiritually (Luke 2:52). We also grow in some ways that aren't so obvious, like our experiences and our perspectives. Ask students for examples of how they've grown through their experiences. Ask them how their perspective is different from when they were a kid. How do they see the world or cope with problems? Are they more aware of others?

3. What did the students write down for the verses about the kingdom of God? Do they have a good grasp of the kingdom? You'll want to check by discussing if thinking about the kingdom of God is different for them. If you need to talk more about the kingdom of God, check these out—Colossians 1:13, 14; Hebrews 12:28; and Revelation 1:6.

4. It's easy to emphasize one aspect of the kingdom of God over another when teaching it to students. Some see the kingdom as an inward and personal reality that connects to the future kingdom, while others emphasize the action side of the kingdom of God. This list incorporates both, modeling the balanced ideal that the kingdom is a spiritual reality that requires us to serve the hurting and outcast as Jesus did. Run through it to see how your students responded.

5. Tell students that the kingdom of God is not just about the future, but we can live in it now. Challenge the students to live by faith, trusting that the King is also their heavenly father who asks us to participate in the mission and purpose of the kingdom.

CLOSE

Close by having a prayer time for your group. Remind students that the kingdom of God is a spiritual kingdom centering on Jesus Christ and his power. So prayer is important as we talk and listen to the King. Have a time of silent prayer when students can pray for opportunities to put their answers to question #5 into practice this week. After a minute or so, a leader can close with a prayer for the group.

MORE

• **A mustard seed is about half the size of the head of a pin and produces a plant (herb) that grows 10 to 12 feet high. Locate a short video on the Internet that shows, in stop action, a seed growing. Search on www.youtube. com or www.google.com for "seed sprouting."**

• **Have students read Luke 4:43 where Jesus declares he was sent specifically to preach the good news of the kingdom of God. The people of that day confused his message with their hope for a political kingdom (Daniel 2:44; Matthew 5:19-20; Mark 10:35-45; Luke 8:1; John 6:15; Acts 1:6; Romans 14:15; and Revelation 19:11-16).**

1. What is your favorite meal? Construct an ideal meal by circling one item in each line below:

JESUS PROVIDES
The feeding of the 5,000
(John 6:5-15)

First course:	Tossed salad	Coleslaw	Cornbread	
	Fresh fruit	Soup		
Veggie:	Corn	Green beans	Peas	
	Asparagus	Carrots		
Starch:	Fries	Baked potato	Rice	
	Rolls	Crackers		
Main:	More veggies	Chicken	Fish	
	Steak	Pizza		
Drink:	Pepsi/Coke	Sprite	Mountain Dew	
	Milk	Fresh juice		
Dessert:	Cake	Fruit pie	Ice cream	Chocolate	Custard

2. Read through the passage again. Describe what Philip was thinking:

What do you think Andrew's perspective was?

3. Jesus asks Philip, "Where shall we buy bread for these people to eat?" Put a check next to which of the following best explains why Jesus tests Philip with this question.

_____ Jesus didn't know how to feed them.

_____ Since Philip was from Bethsaida, a nearby town, he knew where to get food.

_____ Jesus wanted to show that it was not possible to do this by human effort.

_____ Jesus was testing Philip to see if Philip knew that only through God could this be done.

4. What do you do when you're facing a big task or responsibility with a lot of pressure? For each one below, put a Y for "That's like me," an N for "That's not like me," or a D for "It depends on the situation."

_____ I get busy and distracted with something else and end up putting off what I need to do.

_____ I ignore the issue and hope it will go away.

_____ I delay doing it and watch TV, play video games, get online, and spend time with friends.

_____ I try to get someone else to do it for me or help me with it.

_____ I usually think I can't do it or do it well, so I have a hard time caring.

_____ I'm usually overwhelmed—it feels too big to me.

_____ I work through it step by step until it is done.

_____ I like challenges.

_____ I pray about it before taking it on.

_____ I pray about it when things get difficult.

5. This story shows Christ's compassion and his ability to provide. Identify ways you can rely more on God and think less about doing things in your own strength this week.

THIS WEEK

One of the most familiar of Jesus' miracles, the feeding of the five thousand, shows Jesus' great love and provision for people. This TalkSheet connects students' lives with the reality that God is their provider and what that looks like in their lives.

OPENER

One of the best ways to bring life to familiar stories is to help students experience what it might've been like to be there. In order to reenact the scene, you may want to encourage students to come to your meeting a bit hungry by skipping the previous meal. Be as creative as you want. Have a few people be the disciples and come up and bring the food out to the students from the front. For food, use bread, cheese, and bologna. Two people can read the passage as students reflect on it and, during reflection time, have the disciples serve paper bowls of food from behind a small table with a cloth on it. When done, ask students to imagine what it must have been like to have food provided for them. What would it have been like to see such a large crowd fed in such a way?

DISCUSSION

1. Have students share their meal selections. What was the most common meal choice for your group? Did anyone pick asparagus or something else unusual? What wasn't on the "students' favorites" menu?

2. This is the only miracle, besides the resurrection, that's in all of the four Gospels. Why is this a significant event? What does it say about who Jesus is? Ask students what they think the disciples were thinking. Philip and Andrew are specifically mentioned—what are their concerns?

3. Philip was from a nearby town, so it made sense that Jesus asked him instead of the others. John writes in verse 6 that this was a test, but it also showed that this wasn't going to be done though human effort, but would be a testimony of God's ability to provide. How does God want to be the provider in our lives?

4. What did the students notice while working through these? Which one was the hardest to be honest about? Did God's ability to provide play a part in your thinking of how to answer? If God were answering these for you, which answer(s) would he want to change? Ask some students to give examples of moments when they handled a large responsibility really well. We will never be able to rid our lives of pressure or big responsibility, but we can choose how we respond in those moments.

5. Encourage your students to think about how they start their day each morning. Do they focus on just getting through the day, or on how much they can get from the day? What would happen if they started each morning by committing the day to God, trusting him as they walked through the day?

CLOSE

It's easy to see challenging situations through human eyes, measuring them in light of our own experiences, understanding, and worries and fears. What if God wanted to do something amazing in our lives? How would we know? Would we trust him enough to let him use us? Stop and summarize the session, checking whether your middle schoolers understand. Ask, "What did you hear today?" or "What's the big idea from today?" As a few students share, ask if anyone wants to build on earlier answers. Spending a few minutes in review is helpful.

MORE

• **A variation on the opener would be to customize a table ahead of time with a hole in the top and a sheet over the top, cutting a flap in it where the hole would be. Place a person under the table beforehand with some pizzas. Reenact the scene from the Bible story, but contemporize it—have the student playing the child with the lunch possess a pizza instead of fish and bread. Have the "disciples" bring the "kid" and his pizza (in a large customized pizza box) up to the front, put it over the hole in the table and lift up the lid so it blocks the students' view. The pizza box should have the bottom pre-cut and re-taped so that the leader can have pizza slices handed up to them by the person hiding under the table. The effect should be that many pizza slices come out of the table and provide enough pizza for all. Students will eventually figure it out, of course, and this provides a great opportunity for discussion. Remind students that what Jesus did was a true miracle, not a trick—look at what the crowd of more than 5,000 wanted to do with Christ (verse 15).**

1. **Which of the following are miracles? Put "Y" (yes), "D" (depends), or "N" (not a miracle).**

___ A baby is born.

___ You get to school safely on the bus.

___ You get an "A" on a test after not studying at all.

___ Someone has cancer one week and it's gone the next week.

___ A kid has a temper at age 6, but doesn't at age 15.

___ An approaching storm goes around a small town.

2. **Check out Matthew 15:29-31. List the various healings Jesus performed.**

3. **Now, look up Mark 8:22-26. What does it say the man could do once Jesus healed him?**

Look at verses 18 and 19. What does Jesus mean by saying the disciples couldn't see?

4. **Which of the following are descriptions of someone who believes God can help?**

___ A friend shares a big problem with you and you give her a lot of advice.

___ Sally doesn't study for a test, but then prays all morning for a good grade.

___ The airline says all the flights are full, so you make other arrangements.

___ Robert gets up and prays through the day, asking God to guide his thoughts and actions.

___ Meleia lets you know about some big fears she has, and you stop and pray with her for God to help.

___ James is bullied by another guy at school, but prays for the bully to accept Christ.

5. **It's easy to forget that God has amazing power and wants us to be dependent on him. List one or two ways you can work to trust God more and begin relying on him.**

THIS WEEK

Al Michaels' famous question from the 1980 Winter Olympics was, "Do you believe in miracles?" And then he answered it "Yes!" The truth is that many don't believe miracles can happen—that what we see is all there is. Your middle schoolers are growing up in a time where self-reliance and technological advances give the illusion that we can be in control of our lives. While movies and television regularly broadcast themes of ghosts, the paranormal, and mystical religions, most Christians can function with little expectation that God will intervene miraculously. This TalkSheet will get your students discussing that very issue.

OPENER

Assemble a collection of tabloid and online articles about "miraculous" events. Print or cut out the articles from the tabloids (make sure the content is appropriate for your middle schoolers). Divide your students into groups of at least four and give each group two stories. As they read them, they're to create natural explanations for the stories that show they really weren't miracles. Once all the groups are finished, have a person from each group stand and share their group's two stories and the possible explanations. Clarify with each representative as needed so that each summary is clear.

Once every group has shared, transition by discussing whether students think miracles happened in Bible times. Why or why not? Do you think miracles are possible today? Why or why not? Have any of your students heard about or seen a miracle?

DISCUSSION

1. This is an indirect way to get at a definition of *miracle*. What has to happen for something to be called a miracle? Discuss the examples that received the widest range of answers. To stretch their thinking, ask why *all* of them shouldn't be answered "D" for depends. What would it depend on? Take the stance of the farmer outside of town whose farm was hit by the storm. What would his or her opinion be of the storm?

2. What types of problems did people present to Jesus? Help students unpack their answers. What was he healing, and what could the people now do? Have any of your students seen someone healed?

3. The giving of sight in the Bible was very real for those Jesus healed, but it's also symbolic of the moment when believers understand who Jesus is and receive him as their Savior. Ask your students what it was like when they first understood who Jesus is. What did they answer for the second question? Some think that the miracle was done in two steps so that Jesus could illustrate what the disciples were like.

4. How did your students determine which were people who believed God could help? Propose this question: "What if you *knew* God would do a miracle in each case—what would change about each one?" Make sure to discuss the problems inherent with Sally's lack of studying.

5. What does relying on God look like in everyday life for a middle schooler? Brainstorm some ways and list them on the board. Are there things your students need to be praying for that only a miracle of God can fix?

CLOSE

Take some time to summarize the key points from the discussion. Remind students that Jesus never wanted his followers to go it alone, but that they were to depend on him as their shepherd. Tell students that even John the Baptist needed to know if Jesus was the messiah. His followers reported to him all the miracles that Jesus had done. It fit perfectly with the Old Testament prophecy in Isaiah, "They will see the glory of the LORD, the splendor of our God…Be strong, do not fear; your God will come…he will come to save you. Then will the eyes of the blind be opened and the ears of the deaf unstopped. Then will the lame leap like a deer and the mute tongue shout for joy" (taken from Isaiah 35:1-6).

Close in a time of prayer for your students. You may want to have them stand if they want to have more of God in their lives each day.

MORE

• **Numerous sports videos or movies show miraculous finishes—for example, the Miracle on Ice hockey game in the 1980 Olympics. Probably the most dramatic was the Cal versus Stanford game in 1982 (www.youtube.com/watch?v=1Ka2TWrAdqU) or the Trinity versus Millsap game (www.youtube.com/watch?v=gHbzQoXuxdU). Show the clip and discuss whether these can be considered miracles. What would make them a miracle?**

• **It would be well worth it to find two or three people who have experienced a miraculous work in their lives—people who'd connect well with students. It doesn't have to be sensational, just a clear moment when God stepped in and a miracle took place. Have each person share for three minutes about what happened. Ask them how their lives have changed since that moment. You can let students ask some questions, if appropriate. Close by asking students what this says about God. What do these people say about God?**

1. Give a definition for faith.

2. Describe the worst storm you've ever seen or been in.

STEPPING OUT OF THE BOAT

Jesus and Peter walk on the water

(Matthew 14:22-36)

What feelings did you have when you saw it?

3. Read Matthew 14:25-33. Write a one-sentence headline that summarizes what happened in this scene.

4. Do you "A" (agree) or "D" (disagree)?

_____ The men on the boat were frightened.
_____ Peter could've walked on the water without the presence of Jesus.
_____ Peter let his fear of the waves get in the way of his faith in Christ.
_____ If you were there, you would've been able to step out of the boat and walk.

5. You're in a small boat on a big lake, the wind is howling, and the boat is swaying violently from side to side. What do you do?

❏ Pray like crazy.

❏ Hide in the bottom of the boat.

❏ Try to grab the wheel to steer the boat.

❏ Get really sick.

6. Name a recent step of faith you've taken toward Jesus.

Name one stormy area of your life that distracts you from following Jesus.

27. STEPPING OUT OF THE BOAT—Jesus and Peter walk on the water *(Matthew 14:22-36)*

THIS WEEK

Peter's relationship with Jesus was quite a journey—sometimes Peter got it right and other times he didn't. Middle schoolers can relate to Peter's ups and downs as they try to do what God wants them to do. This Talk-Sheet follows Peter as he steps out of a boat in faith to walk on the water toward Jesus, sinks as he focuses on the wind and waves, and is lifted up from the water by Christ. This TalkSheet will help those among your teens who may feel as though they've also taken steps toward God but are sinking and need God to lift them up.

OPENER

This is a great opportunity to do some trust-building activities. The Trust Fall is a classic, but may not work for most middle school groups due to its requirements for strength and its risk level. You can do The Trust Lean and other exercises found at wilderdom.com/games/TrustActivities.html. A good low-risk activity that builds group unity and yet demands trust among the participants is a Sitting Circle. Have your students stand in a circle and face right so they're standing front to back in a tight circle. Have them hold the person's waist in front of them and, at your signal, slowly bend their knees until each person is sitting on the front part of the lap of the person behind them. The circle should be standing on its own. If you can't get it the first time, you may want to try again and make sure students are not too far apart. Once you achieve a sitting circle, ask your students to raise their arms as a group. To challenge them more, have them take a simultaneous step forward with their right foot.

When done, have everyone stand slowly and return to their spots. Discuss how students felt when they trusted their peers to hold them up. How did it take faith to make the circle work? In whom or what did students have faith? Use this activity to propel students' thinking about faith.

DISCUSSION

1. Get your students to share their definitions. How many of them were spiritual in nature? Suggest some actions and have students discuss how or why they take "faith"—turning on a light, sitting in a chair, giving a speech in school, or parachuting.
2. Have students share their "storm stories." This will take some time, so limit the length of sharing for each student. Let as many students share as possible.
3. What headlines did your students write? Get as many answers as possible—and have fun with this.

4. Read each one of the first three and ask who agreed and who disagreed. This will give you a chance to talk about what it must have been like that early morning.
5. Assign each answer to a different corner of the room and have students move to the corner for their answer. Have them talk with others in their corner about why they picked that answer. Have someone from each group share why most people in their group answered the way they did.
6. Have students look at question #4 and their last answer. Challenge students that God may want them to get out of the boat and take a bold step in some area of their lives. Remind students that they don't have to go through stormy times alone—they can connect with a parent or Christian adult who can help them.

CLOSE

So what's the moral of the story? Is it (a) keep your eyes on Jesus, (b) get out of the boat and take bold steps, or (c) trust that God can calm your storms? Peter had the faith to get out of the boat, but then he started doubting. Remind students that we may desire to follow Christ, but sometimes find ourselves doubting or sinking—yet Christ is capable of lifting us up. Our stormy areas can become opportunities to demonstrate our faith in God. Have students bow their heads and read the prayer in Psalm 144:7-9: "Reach down your hand from on high; deliver me and rescue me from the mighty waters, from the hands of foreigners whose mouths are full of lies, whose right hands are deceitful. I will sing a new song to you, my God."

MORE

• **You may want to go online and find a short storm video to show. Use it to kick off your session or to talk with your students about storms. How often do storms come along? What effect do storms have on our lives? Do we get more fearful or do we want to trust God more? Is it difficult to believe God is in control during a storm?**

• **For more on faith, have students read James 2:14-26. Discuss how what we do connects with what we believe. Why did Peter get out of the boat? Romans 4:18-25 shows how Abraham acted in faith, a key part of Hebrews 11:8-16. What do these verses explain about Abraham's faith?**

• **Is faith a blind step, or is it based on something you know? Does it take faith to believe that Abraham Lincoln existed? That men walked on the moon? That Jesus is who he says he is? On what do people base their beliefs? Does it take faith to not believe in God?**

1. For each line below, circle the choice that best defines who you are.

Football, Tennis, Swimming, Basketball, Baseball, Auto Racing

Beach, Mall, Ski Slope, Swimming Pool, Garage, Woods, Field

iPod, mp3, email, blogs, DVD, IM

Hip-hop, Jazz, Country, Electronica, Pop, Alternative, Christian

New York, Florida, Chicago, San Diego, Vancouver, Denver

I AM
The seven "I Am" statements of Jesus
(John 6:35; 8:12; 10:7-9, 11-14; 11:25-26; 14:6; 15:1, 5)

2. Pick three of the following verses and fill in the words Jesus used to describe himself—and then give an example of what it means.

VERSE	WHO JESUS IS	WHAT IT MEANS
John 6:35		
John 8:12		
John 10:7-9		
John 10:11-14		
John 11:25		
John 14:6		
John 15:5		

3. Pick two of the "I Am" statements you answered and think about how you'd explain what they mean to a friend. Write out a sentence that helps a friend know more about Jesus based on these two "I Am" statements.

4. Think of something (object, title, activity) that best illustrates what Jesus is in your life. Put that in the first blank and then complete the sentence. You can do more than one, if you feel creative!

Jesus is the _____ for me, because he _____.

THIS WEEK

Jesus was more than just a prophet or a great moral teacher; his listeners understood clearly that Jesus claimed to be God. We get to see this understanding developing when Jesus revealed more about who he was to those who followed him. In this TalkSheet session, your students will discuss Jesus' "I Am" statements and how they give us examples of who Jesus is.

OPENER

Find the movie *The Gospel of John* and show the scene from the end of John 8 where Jesus is teaching the people about who he is. The clip should end just after the narrator reports that Jesus disappeared. What do your students notice about this scene? What was Jesus really saying when he said, "I am"? What did the people understand that Jesus was claiming? Read Exodus 3:14 and Philippians 2:6. Jesus made specific claims about who he was. Today we're going to look at those claims and discuss how they affect our lives today.

DISCUSSION

1. Have students get in groups of four and share their answers. How do words like this help people know more about us? How are they limited in describing who we are?
2. Have students stay in groups and talk about their answers. (They can fill in any boxes with answers from others for lines they didn't complete.) Have a copy of this on an overhead or whiteboard and ask students to share their answers. Record answers in the boxes on the overhead. Which of these were new to your students? Which make the most sense? Which are unclear?

> **Bread of life**—spiritual nourishment, not from external sources in this world, but from Jesus.
> **Light of the world**—shows us the correct path. For more, see 1 John 1:6-7.
> **The gate/door**—only through Jesus can we have spiritual sanctuary or salvation.
> **The Good Shepherd**—he cares for and protects the flock. See Isaiah 40:11.
> **The resurrection and life**—Jesus gives eternal life. See John 5:24 and 10:28.
> **The way, truth, and life**—salvation is not through many ways, but through Christ alone.
> **The vine**—we are to be connected and bear fruit.

3. It's often hard to explain spiritual concepts to children, but it's helpful in getting students to think about the "so what?" factor. Ask students to share what they wrote. Some will have done this easily and others will have struggled. Let students volunteer to share.
4. Have your students think over the "I Am" statements Jesus made. Why can Jesus make these statements? Why did Jesus use word pictures to communicate deep truths? Encourage them to look over their responses. Do you think God still wants to communicate with people in relevant ways? How does he do that? What's our part in that relationship?

CLOSE

It's easy to get in a routine and lose sight of who Jesus said he was. These statements show the power and place Jesus has in the world. More than merely someone who lived in the past, Jesus' "I Am" statements show he's alive and in power today—and middle schoolers need to consider the place Jesus has in their lives today. As they look over the "I Am" statements, show them how these statements are relational and not impersonal. Walk through each of these with your middle schoolers and have them think of ways each statement can be true in their lives today. How can Jesus be that "I Am" for them now?

MORE

• **Kick off the night by having middle schoolers create their own superheros. (Do a Google search for "make your own superhero" and from those Web sites develop a page of suitable ideas from which students can select and develop their own superheros.) Let them introduce themselves to the whole group or just to those around them. Discuss the differences between the imaginary characters and the prophets in the Old Testament. When Jesus came, people were unsure who he was—some believed and others doubted (Matthew 28:17). Jesus used metaphors to help people understand who he is.**

• **Jesus was described with many names in the New Testament. Give these verses to students and discuss the meanings of the names given to Jesus: Matthew 9:27 and 11:19; Ephesians 2:20; Hebrews 1:2-3; 1 Peter 2:4-5 and 5:4; 1 John 2:1; and finally, Revelation 1:8 and 17:14. Which one is new to students? Which one do they think is the most significant? Conclude by connecting the meanings to students' current situations. Christ wants to rule in their lives now, and these descriptions demonstrate his power and ability to do that.**

1. **Who do people say Jesus is? Check all the things you've heard people say:**

___ The big guy upstairs.
___ A man who is just all right with me.
___ The Son of God.
___ A made-up person.
___ Savior and Lord.
___ A great moral teacher.
___ One of many gods.
___ Too confusing to think about.
___ The Son of Man.
___ An example of how we should live.

"YOU ARE THE CHRIST!"

Peter's confession

(Matthew 16:13-19)

2. **Read Matthew 16:13-19. Who does Peter say Jesus is?**

Who does Jesus say Peter is?

3. **Give a short definition of these terms from verse 16:**

Messiah -

Son of the living God -

4. **Below is a list of important functions in the church. Circle the ones that are meaningful to you. Put a checkmark next to the ones that are important, but not meaningful to you.**

Teaching and preaching	Group prayer	Being with Christian friends
Communion or Eucharist	Worship through music	Baptism
Potluck dinners	Liturgy	Mission trips and service projects
Retreats and camps	Dramas and musicals	Giving and tithing
Support missions	Community involvement	Traditional music
Bible study	Small groups	Being with God

5. **How has the church helped you grow in your faith? Put a checkmark next to areas where the church has helped you learn or grow.**

Understanding the Bible _____
How to share my faith _____
How to obey God _____
How to grow in my relationship with Jesus _____

Knowing more about who Jesus is _____
Understanding who the Holy Spirit is _____
How to reach out to others _____
How to handle my problems _____

29. "YOU ARE THE CHRIST!"—Peter's confession *(Matthew 16:13-19)*

THIS WEEK

Pop quizzes. We don't know when they're coming, but they show how much we really know—or don't. Jesus turns to his disciples and gives them a pop quiz about who he is. Many in Jesus' time were trying to figure out who he was, and the disciples were no different. Sometimes they understood, but other times they missed the mark. Peter aced the quiz and Jesus responded with some profound declarations, which are the focus of this TalkSheet.

OPENER

Make a handout of 10 trivia questions. Get two or three from contemporary news headlines of the week, two or three from a Bible trivia Web page, and three or four historical questions found online. Divide the students into four equal groups and pass out the handout to each group. Give each group three minutes to fill in the answers. Next, give the correct answers and ask them to grade their own, with a prize to the winning group. Ask students how they learn new information—books, friends, television, Internet, or school. How do they decide what's important to know? Ask students if they ever feel overloaded with all of the information that's out there.

DISCUSSION

1. Discover which of the answers your group found most prominent. For some humor, share a handful of children's quotes about Jesus and the Bible from www.innocentenglish.com/funny-bloopers-mistakes-quotes/church-bible-mistakes.html.
2. Jesus' message was prophetic, so people tried to discern whether Jesus was truly a prophet. He was more than a prophet, however—he was Immanuel, "God with us," a fulfillment of the prophecies. This was difficult for many in Jesus' day to accept. Discuss with students various reasons that Jesus gave Peter his name and called him the "rock."
3. Peter had said something like this before (John 6:69). What did Peter mean by "Messiah"? What does "Son of the Living God" mean?
4. Jesus says he'll build his church on Peter's commitment. What does he mean by "church"? What is the purpose of the church? What should be the purpose of the church? Does Acts 2:42 give any helpful hints? Peter wrote about the church later (1 Peter 1:1 and 2:9). What functions of the church connect most with your students? Pay attention to their answers and try to draw out some good discussion about what the church does.
5. Refer students to verse 19. The person who held the keys controlled who entered or didn't enter a home. In the same way, Jesus says that the church (us) is the way people will hear about, and be able to enter, the kingdom of God (Matthew 23:13 illustrates the opposite). How did your students learn what obeying God looks like? How did they learn how to handle problems? Did anyone have a hard time selecting one?

CLOSE

Remind your students that the church is not a man-made institution, but something that Christ himself created and has given authority to. What does it mean that the church has authority? Write these words in a column on the left side of the board: Building Community, Teaching, Baptizing, Obeying, Evangelism, and Making Disciples. Discuss with students how the church accomplishes each of these and generate a list of ideas to the right. Are there other purposes for church? Ask students if they think they're a part of the church. If so, what's their job, as the church, in each of these areas? Close by discussing how your youth group, as the church, reflects these values to those who come.

If you have the time and the necessary closeness in your group, this may be an opportunity to sit down for a discussion about the role of church in the lives of your middle schoolers. The middle school years can be a very difficult time for students to connect with church. Ask students to talk about church, but don't correct any answers—the goal here is to have them share openly and honestly about their feelings toward church. Close by sharing your own experiences as a middle schooler, and encourage them to see church as something more than their local building and people—it's something God is building around the world.

MORE

• **If you want to add to the session, take a video camera out for "man on the street" interviews, asking them who Jesus is. Edit together the better answers and show a three-to-four-minute video from that. You'll have better quality if you use a camera and a handheld microphone instead of relying on the camera's microphone. Try to select an area where you can conduct the interviews without problems and where you'll get a wide variety of answers from local people.**

• **Do most people in churches today understand most of the words and phrases pastors and others use? Ask students if there are concepts or phrases regularly talked about in churches that they don't understand. You may want to pass out slips of paper and have students write them down. You can answer some of them, create an online wiki for your group, or devote a whole meeting to this.**

1. Describe one or two times when you've climbed to a high point. What did it take to get there? What did you see?

MOUNTAINTOP SURPRISE
The transfiguration
(Mark 9:2-10)

2. What have been the best highlights of your life? Under each category, fill in the two or three greatest moments.

MY SOCIAL LIFE   MY ACTIVE LIFE   MY SPIRITUAL LIFE

3. If you were called on at school to write a sentence introducing Jesus to those who don't know anything about him, what would you say? Write it down.

4. Read Mark 9:2-5. Which of the following best describes Peter's response?

___ He was scared and didn't know what to do, but he had to say something.

___ He wanted to stay there and keep the wonderful experience going.

___ He thought Christ's kingdom had come and that three churches were needed.

5. Read Mark 9:7-9. The voice of God said, "Listen to him." What does that mean?

6. Imagine you're walking off the mountain with the three disciples. What new thoughts about Jesus would you have?

THIS WEEK

Up and down—that's how the Christian life can feel sometimes to a middle school student. If they're not on a high, then it can be easy to think things aren't going well spiritually. Though there can be deep valleys of uncertainty that challenge their ability to follow faithfully, the mountaintop experiences also present problems in that the kids think they're normal. The reality is that it can actually be more difficult to maintain a consistent relationship with God when things are going well. They can get self-sufficient, ignoring God and his Holy Spirit in their lives. This session uses the transfiguration of Christ to help students discuss these ups and downs in their lives.

OPENER

Kick off the meeting by talking about roller coasters. What are your students' favorites? Who loves them? Who's a bit scared of them? Some will be scared, so don't let others make fun of them! If you have the equipment, project a roller coaster simulation from a computer game or online (go to www.youtube.com and type in "roller coaster POV" for some examples—and make sure to preview). Ask students to give you ideas to complete this sentence: "Life is like a roller coaster because _____."

To start the discussion, have a fast-paced brainstorming discussion on the topic of "feeling close to God." Tell students that youth leaders sometimes hear people say, "I don't feel like I have a close relationship with God." What do they mean by this? Have any of your students said this before? What do they mean by the word *feel*? Does it mean they've been cut off from God? Can a person sense (or feel) whether their relationship with God is close or not? What's the danger in relying on our feelings to determine how our relationship with God is doing?

DISCUSSION

1. Move quickly on this one. Get students to share where they've climbed. Any cool views? Ask for a show of hands on who has flown in an airplane. Ask how the world looks different from the perspective of an airplane. Transition by saying that sometimes when we're high up, we can see life differently—get a new perspective. Some things look smaller and some look bigger.

2. Were any highlights easier to come up with than others? Have a few students volunteer their answers. Are they quick to share one column over another? (Ask specifically for their answers under "my spiritual life" if you don't hear any.) Explain that some people call these "mountaintop experiences," a phrase that comes from the story you're looking at in Mark 9:2-10.

3. Let your students share their sentences. What was the focus of their introductions? Keep track of this and briefly summarize those observations before moving on.

4. Peter felt like he had to say something even though he wasn't asked. Have students ever had incredible spiritual experiences that they wanted to extend? Can people be scared even when they're having an amazing spiritual experience with God? Remind students that Christ's transfiguration meant that he changed into his glorified form, the way he'll appear when he comes a second time. Why did seeing him like that produce fear in the disciples?

5. The phrase means "be obedient to Him" (and connects to Deuteronomy 18:15). Why do you think God chooses to say this? What did your students write down in their introductory sentences? Did any of them have something about obedience? Why is obedience a big deal to God when it usually isn't as prominent in our thinking of God?

6. Just like being high off the ground gives us a new perspective, seeing how big (powerful, holy) Jesus is can influence how we see our problems. Do you think the disciples had more confidence in Jesus after this? And yet, after this moment, each of the three disciples still had a down moment. James and John misunderstood Jesus' teaching and fought over who would be the greatest (see TalkSheet #40), Peter denied Jesus (TalkSheet #50), and all three refused to wash the feet of the other disciples (TalkSheet #44). What lessons can we learn? Is it possible to never fall?

CLOSE

How does a mountaintop experience with God transform our lives? Can you have a strong relationship with God without having mountaintop experiences? Can they hurt our relationship with God? Have students reflect on moments in which they had spiritual highlights in their lives. Were these moments connected to planned events, or did they just happen? Close by discussing ways your group can make themselves available for God to do transformational things.

MORE

• **Peter actually reflects about this experience in 1 Peter 1:12-21. As you read this, describe what role this mountaintop experience played in Peter's life. What confidence did it give him? How does he use the experience to both encourage and challenge his readers?**

• **The same reflections that Peter gives his readers in 1 Peter can be achieved by finding several older Christian adults who can share on a panel discussion. Coach them to keep their answers concise, and don't have more than three. Ask them to talk about their own mountaintop experiences. Did these experiences help in their faith in God? What role did those, and the low times, play in their lives? Keep the panel discussion moving.**

1. When you get mad and forgiveness is needed, which of the following are you most like?

____ Judge: I assign penalties to people who wrong me and make them pay.

____ Time bomb: I hold a grudge inside and explode later.

____ Scorekeeper: I keep a record of how people treat me and I know the score.

____ Duck: Stuff that happens to me rolls off my back and I stay afloat.

____ Hugger: I try to avoid conflict, so I forgive quickly.

FORGIVE? FORGET IT!
The unmerciful servant
(Matthew 18:21-35)

2. For each of the following, give your best guess at what you think is true:

Times per week a middle school student gets angry: _____

Percent of middle schoolers who are bitter about something: _____

Percent of people who believe anger will just go away if ignored: _____

Number of people you're mad at that you need to forgive: _____

3. Read Matthew 18:21. Rewrite Peter's question to reflect what you think Peter is really asking.

4. Read Matthew 18:23-30. Which of the following best explains why the first servant wasn't willing to forgive the second servant who owed him so little?

____ He wasn't truly grateful for being forgiven.

____ He was greedy—wanting more money made him act the way he did.

____ He just worked for the Master—he didn't want to *be* like him.

____ His angry personality just got the best of him.

5. Look at these two verses and rewrite them so they describe what true forgiveness is.

Colossians 3:13—

Ephesians 4:32—

THIS WEEK

Some conflict in life is unavoidable. So are moments when we disobey God. The issue isn't whether they happen, it's how we respond when they do. Anger, bitterness, sarcasm ("anger on simmer"), and envy seem all too common today, even among middle schoolers and churches. This TalkSheet provides many opportunities to discuss forgiveness, but the real goal is to get students to implement what they already know about forgiveness. This week it would be helpful to read the Bible story before students begin their TalkSheets.

OPENER

Ask students to think of a time when they behaved badly or made a big mistake and were forgiven for it. Remind students not to share the specific details about what happened. Ask them what it felt like to be in a situation where they've done something wrong and then been forgiven. Did other people truly forgive them? How did they know they were forgiven? Do people forgive more easily today than when their parents were young? Why or why not? Remind students that we're all in need of forgiveness—and that part of Jesus' mission to this earth was to offer and model God's forgiveness for sin.

DISCUSSION

1. Divide the students into five groups, one for each answer. Have the students in each group discuss why they chose that description. Let them talk for about five minutes and then draw their attention back to you. Have them brainstorm reasons why people react to conflict in different ways. Take note of which group was largest and which was smallest. Then let students return to their original spots.

2. Have students share their answers to the first three, going through them one at a time to see if there's a consensus among your students. Would your students say there's a lot of anger and hurt among their friends? Is that different for adults? It's important to let your students know that anger that isn't dealt with won't go away. What does this say for those who choose to bottle up their feelings? Discuss steps in dealing with bitterness and anger (1 Peter 3:9). Let the fourth one go for now.

3. Is there a limit to how many times your students should have to forgive someone else? Is there ever a situation where they don't have to forgive someone else?

4. The larger sum of money was equal to well over $12 million today. The smaller amount was about $20. Which of the reasons listed did your students select? How are these four similar to reasons why people don't forgive others?

5. How did your students describe forgiveness? What reason do these verses give for why we must forgive?

CLOSE

Most people are aware of Jesus' teaching on forgiveness. The trick isn't to have a good discussion about it, as you've done today, but rather to put it into practice in everyday life. Did your students identify a situation in question #2 where they need to work toward forgiving another person? What keeps them from putting forgiveness into practice? What are the common barriers to forgiveness? Is forgiveness an important part of being like Jesus? Close by sharing a story from your own life of when forgiveness made a difference and showed you and others a bit about who God is.

MORE

• **This session would be fun to introduce with a melodrama. Find three students with dramatic flair and have them act out the story as you read it, repeating the quotes after you read them. You'll need a couple of extra people to be the other servants. When finished, ask students what they noticed in the story.**

• **Do some research and try to find a TV show with a scene on forgiveness. After showing the scene, ask students how realistic it was. What issue needed forgiveness? What factors kept forgiveness from being easy?**

• **For more on God as the God of forgiveness, have students connect with Nehemiah 9:17; Psalm 103:12; Isaiah 43:25; and Jeremiah 31:34. Writers point out that the teaching at that time was to forgive someone three times. It's possible Peter got the notion of "seventy times seven" from Proverbs 24:16 and Amos 2:1.**

1. What's a missionary? Write a definition below:

Do you want to go on a short-term mission trip in the future? Why or why not?

2. Which of the following is a missionary? Check all that apply.

_____ Carla stays at home after school and prays for her neighbors.
_____ Jayson intentionally goes to an alternative school so he can be a witness to students.
_____ Tammy spends a month in Romania to work in an orphanage.
_____ The Sanchez family chooses to sponsor a child through Compassion International.
_____ Devon invites his friends to youth group and helps them get there.

3. Read Luke 10:2-4. Write down two or three things that someone who worked in a field would do.

Describe how a lamb would act if it were among wolves:

4. Read Luke 10:8-9. What did Jesus tell them to say?

5. Read verses 17-20. What would you have felt if you'd just seen all of this happen—and then Jesus told you to be more joyful since your name was written in heaven?

6. Think of a place where missionaries go to serve. List three words that describe that location.

Do these words also describe your current place in life? Next to each word put a "T" for "True for my world" or "N" for "Not true for my world."

THIS WEEK

Short-term missions trips (or service projects) have become so common that some observers have called them a movement or a phenomenon. Though short-term mission trips are more common among high school youth groups, most middle schoolers are familiar with what they are. People who participate in them often say they're the most significant experiences in their life. Service, missions, and youth ministry continue to provide opportunities for your students to learn that the Christian faith isn't something to be lived in secret. Instead, we are commanded (Matthew 28:18-20) to go into the entire world and teach and care for others, speaking as witnesses about what Christ has done. Using a story of an event that looked like a short-term mission trip, this TalkSheet can serve as a springboard to discuss missions and the roles your students can have.

OPENER

Find out all the mission and service efforts your church or organization supports or performs each year. Write them on a sheet of paper or whiteboard before the meeting, or make it more fun by having a short game in a TV game show format to see if your students are aware of what their church is doing already. Make sure to include overseas and local ministry efforts. As your students consider this list, discuss the purposes of the various ministries. Are they all the same? Ask what students think the mission of your group is. What should their role be in their community? In local schools? The world?

DISCUSSION

1. What definitions did they come up with? Do they center on the gospel? Do they include help and service in areas other than just spiritual matters? Ask your students where they learned about missions.
2. Who was the missionary according to your students? Expand the question by asking how each of these is part of a missionary movement. See if the students have a wide or narrow understanding of what a missionary is. Do missionaries have to serve overseas? Do they have to be full time to be real missionaries?
3. How does the image of a harvest field help us understand more about ministry? What about "lambs among wolves?" Remind students of the stories in Acts of the persecution faced by the early disciples. You may want to discuss what opposition your students face when they try to take a stand for God.

4. Tell students that Jesus sent his followers out on short mission experiences as his representatives. What did they tell others as they ministered to them? Discuss with students how a kingdom grows. How does the kingdom of God grow in their area?
5. You don't have to ask for student answers here. This question reveals the tension of ministry—we often lose sight of whose ministry it is. So we do good things, go on short-term mission trips, and seek out moments where we get a good feeling or have a good experience—rather than seek out ministry because God leads us as he expands his kingdom. Remind students of "lambs among wolves." That's not a place most people would want to be today!
6. Have students comment on their description and how it fits in their lives. Do these things have to be present for it to be a mission field? Can their neighborhood be a mission field? How are other mission fields different?

CLOSE

Ask students this question: If it were clear that God was calling you to reach out to another group of people, would you be willing to do that? What if it meant being a full-time missionary somewhere else? Jesus began his ministry with the declaration that the kingdom of God was now here (Mark 1:15). What are ways students can work to expand that in their schools? What can they specifically do as a youth group to participate in God's mission around the world? Ask students to close their eyes and reflect, pray, or just sit and think about their role in God's kingdom. After a minute, read Luke 10:2-3 and pray for your students.

MORE

• If your group has students who have been on mission trips, prearrange to have a panel discussion about missions with them. Give them the questions ahead of time, remind them to keep their answers short, and coach them about what makes a good panel discussion (they can be quite bad otherwise). Focus on the actual work of the trip, not the effect on their lives. Other questions can focus on how the trip helped them understand missions and what their future involvement in missions and service will be.

WHO IS THE ACCUSER?
Jesus rescues the woman caught in adultery
(John 8:1-11)

1. Which adult in your house (mom, dad, others) is the tough one?

When you were seven or eight years old and got in trouble, how were you punished?

2. When were you last mad at someone? Write down the first names of as many people as you can remember that you've been mad at in the last two or three weeks.

How did you fix those relationships? Are you still mad at any of the people?

3. Do you think some sins are worse than others? Why or why not?

4. Read John 8:1-8. When Jesus said that those without sin could throw the first stone, what do you think he meant?

❏ No one is without sin, so no one should judge and punish others.

❏ Everyone is a sinner, so shouldn't we stone others, too?

❏ Many of you in the crowd have also committed sexual sins.

❏ Haven't you heard what I've been teaching?

❏ God is establishing a new law that focuses on deliverance.

5. Read verses 9-11. Once the woman heard Jesus' response, what do you think she thought or felt?

6. Read Revelation 12:10. Who is our accuser, and what does he do?

7. Today we don't carry stones in our hands, but what are some examples of how we still judge others?

THIS WEEK

Some people have the mistaken perspective that God is out to get them. Rather than seeing God as one who offers forgiveness through repentance, they see God as one who gets mad every time they mess up. The Bible shows that while God is holy and cares about our obedience, he's also gracious and quick to forgive. This is an important concept for middle schoolers to grasp early in their lives because they often wrestle with shame—and sometimes adults are quick to shame them for a variety of extrabiblical reasons. This TalkSheet helps students see Christ's compassion and grace in action and discover that the Bible tells us that Satan is actually the accuser.

Be sensitive and alert during this TalkSheet—some of your students may have a history of being abused by a parent, and some may be in abusive situations of varying degrees right now. You may hear a comment that you need to follow up on privately and talk to your pastor for assistance.

OPENER

Have students go to the middle of the room. Next, have them move to the left or right side of the room—whichever side best reflects their opinions of the following questions.

Do most Christian middle school students feel good about their relationship with God (to their right) *or do they have a lot of shame and doubt* (left)? Discuss why students chose where to stand. This can generate a lot of discussion, so ask your kids what facts people use to decide how they're doing. Have students move based on these two questions:

Do most middle school students carry a lot of guilt around about stuff they've done in the past (to their right) *or do they feel forgiven and free* (left)? Again, discuss the responses after students move.

When you attend church and/or youth group, do you feel better about your relationship with God (right) *or do you feel more ashamed* (left)? This is a tough one to discuss, but very worthwhile—especially if students are able to accurately reflect on this.

DISCUSSION

1. Ask students if they've learned to "work" their parents. Do they know which one to ask if they want a favorable answer? Do your students get in trouble more now than they did when they were seven or eight years old? Feel free to share a suitable story from your own life where you got in big trouble.
2. How many of your students were mad at three people or fewer? More than seven? Have them raise their hands. Discuss with your students how they resolve

conflicts with friends. It's quite probable that it isn't resolved, and they just let it drop. That's normal for middle schoolers! Now, flip the question—who did they make mad this past week? What have they done to fix those situations? What should they do?
3. Students will have a range of answers from "all sin is sin" to a ranking system. Remind students that all sin is against what God intends. What's the danger in thinking of some sins as little?
4. What do students think Jesus meant? Tell students that Jesus effectively identified everyone in the crowd with the woman and her sin. They understood that at some point in their lives, each of them deserved condemnation as well. Why is it important to not be so proud that we aren't aware of our own ability to disobey God?
5. Ask students about their answers. Do they think she changed her behavior after that encounter? Why or why not?
6. Why do people think God is the accuser? Should Christians feel like God is "out to get them"? Let students know that when we think we're not good enough for God to love us, we need to pause and examine the source of those thoughts.
7. Have students report their answers and list them on the board. Do the verses say we can't take the speck out of others' eyes? How do these verses help us?

CLOSE

It's not uncommon in middle school to feel like a group of people have circled around you, and each is holding a rock ready to throw at you. The rocks may take forms other than a stone—rocks may look more like anger, criticisms, or harsh judgment. It's easy to think God is holding a stone, too—that we'll never be good enough for him to love us. Of course, this story shows that it's not about "earning" God's forgiveness. Discuss with your students how they can receive God's forgiveness and how they can combat feelings that God is accusing them of not being good enough. You may also want to remind them that they're not to act as accusers of others.

MORE

• **The crowd had gathered in judgment of the woman who was caught in adultery. Discuss with students whether they hold others to a higher standard than themselves. Help them think through ways they may act themselves, but they don't let others act that way.**
• **Several other verses show Satan's role as the accuser. Students can check out these Bible passages: Job 1:6-10; Zechariah 3:1-2; John 10:10; and 1 Peter 5:8-9. Based on these verses, what is Satan's job? What's the focus of his accusations?**

1. How do you usually express gratitude/thanks to others?

❏ Card or note   ❏ Give a gift
❏ Thank them face-to-face
❏ Do something nice for them
❏ A big hug   ❏ I'm not very good at it
❏ Other _____

THANKING CHRIST
The 10 lepers
(Luke 17:11-19)

2. Read Luke 17:11-19. Do you think people today are thankful? Why or why not?

3. Check out 1 Thessalonians 5:16-18. Is it possible to be thankful in all situations? Why or why not?

Do we have a choice about whether to be thankful or not?

4. For each person below, write what you're thankful for and the way you can best let that person know your appreciation.

	I AM THANKFUL FOR:	I CAN LET THEM KNOW BEST BY:
Parent		
Friend		
Youth group leader(s)		
Jesus Christ		
Someone else		

THIS WEEK

Gratitude versus selfishness—it's a real battle! It can be difficult for students to reach out much beyond themselves during the middle school years. The mirror, social pressure, and the ever-changing body and mind contribute to an intense self-awareness necessary just to keep it all together during this transition period. The danger is that we can grow to feel as though we're owed certain blessings (such as health, respect, comforts, or fairness)—and consumer forces reinforce those feelings of entitlement. In the midst of this discontent, we fail to realize how much God has already done for us. This TalkSheet allows students to express their thankfulness to God as they learn about Jesus' healing of the 10 lepers.

OPENER

Get a video camera and head out around town to interview people who work in various jobs where people would have the opportunity to express thanks to them. Ask these people how well people express gratitude to them. Some possible people to talk to would include a waitress or waiter, doctor, firefighter, pastor, janitors, hotel personnel, and teacher (and you may think of others). Follow up your question by asking them about the general gratefulness of people they serve. Have someone edit this together into a fast-moving video of less than five minutes and show it at the meeting.

DISCUSSION

1. Have your students share their answers here. Ask some to talk about when they did a great job of expressing gratitude to someone. How long has it been since your students thanked someone else?
2. Students will have a variety of answers for this question. Let them discuss for a while. Then ask students to help you construct a definition of ungratefulness on the board.
3. Ask students in which situations they find it most difficult to be thankful. For example, can they be thankful at school for getting an education even though they may not like school? Can someone be thankful even when circumstances aren't going his or her way? Working from your group's definition of ungratefulness, try to help students see that thankfulness isn't dependent on things going our way.

4. Just as the leper who went back to Jesus modeled for us, we need to pause and make sure to thank those who have provided for us in the past. Ask students what they noticed as they completed this question. Have they done a good job expressing thankfulness or are there some ways they need to communicate their gratitude better?

CLOSE

Jesus met these lepers on the border between Samaria and Galilee (verse 11) as he was going to Jerusalem. At a point between the three communities, Jesus met people in need and healed them (verse 14). One returned and was proclaimed "made well" (verse 19) because of his faith. Tell students that often their ability to be thankful to God, even when they aren't getting their way, can be a powerful demonstration of their faith and trust in Jesus.

Have students look over their answers and help you create a definition of ungratefulness. Write it on the board. Pass out clean sheets of paper and have students write a prayer of thanks from their heart to God or a letter of thanks to a parent (or other guardian) to whom they need to express deep gratitude. Play a song or two and just let students write. Tell them to tuck the prayer in their Bible and put it somewhere in their bedroom later as a reminder. If they wrote a letter, either have them hand deliver it, or give them an envelope to address, and you can mail it for them.

MORE

• **Because of personality differences, different people want to be thanked in the way they prefer to receive affection. These have been called "love languages" by Dr. Gary Chapman. For more, visit www.fivelovelanguages. com/learn.html. Have your students move into an area marked with one of these signs and let them discuss how these connect to giving thanks.**

• **One of the most fundamental problems with thankfulness is often that we aren't thankful for who God created us to be. We don't like how we look, or act, and we spend a lot of time wishing we were like someone else. Let students read Psalm 139:13-16 and discuss with them ways they can learn to be thankful for who they are.**

1. **What do you like best in a friend? Circle the traits that you appreciate in your friends:**

They like the same things
They're always the same
They want to be with me

They live close   They're a lot like me
My parents like them They go to church
They're quiet   They're Christians
They don't smell   They're talkative
They look good   They encourage me
They're funny   They're different from me

UNWRAPPING THE DEAD
Jesus raises Lazarus from the grave
(John 11:1-6, 17-44)

2. **Read John 11:1-7. What did Jesus feel toward Lazarus?**

What did Jesus say would be the end of Lazarus' sickness?

3. **Read verses 21-23 and 32. What is Martha and Mary's complaint to Jesus?**

4. **Read verse 31-37. How do you respond to Jesus' crying at the tomb of a friend?**

  ____ It seems strange to think Jesus cried.

  ____ I think it shows that he cares for people.

  ____ He was crying because of sin and its result in death.

  ____ Since he was also human, he experienced human emotions.

5. **Read verses 38, 39, 43, and 44. Based on Martha's thoughts, describe what the grave clothes must have been like for those asked to take them off Lazarus. Do your best job at describing them.**

35. UNWRAPPING THE DEAD—Jesus raises Lazarus from the grave *(John 11:1-6, 17-44)*

THIS WEEK

A dramatic moment in Jesus' ministry was the raising of Lazarus from the dead. It's a touching scene because it shows Jesus with his friends, a moment that ends with a powerful demonstration that Jesus wasn't just a man, but also God. The range of emotions in the story, from Jesus' grief and compassion to the anger of Martha, will spark your middle schoolers to enter into the story and learn more about who Jesus is—and how they can help "unwrap" others.

OPENER

Open the discussion time by talking about funerals—and please be aware that some of your students may currently be in a period of grief, so be sensitive and don't treat the topic lightly. Ask for a quick show of hands—how many of your middle schoolers have been to a funeral. Ask how many have been to the funeral of a close relative and again have them raise their hands. Let students describe some of the funerals they've attended. How are some funerals different from others? After getting a few answers, discuss the purpose of funerals. Walk through what usually goes on at a funeral and have students think about the purpose behind each part. Move toward a reflective question: Does going to, or thinking about, funerals make you feel closer to or farther from God?

DISCUSSION

1. What traits do your students like in their friends? Discuss with them what they think Jesus' friends were like. This story shows us Jesus with some of his friends. Have students stop and think about their friends. Do they take them for granted or do they try to be a good friend? Have them look through this list and think about which items they do for their friends.
2. People described Lazarus to Jesus as "the one you love." The word here for "love" means "warmly, as a dear friend." Discuss with students how love and friendship mix. Is it too much for middle schoolers to have friends they love? Too much for high schoolers? Adults? The purpose of Lazarus' illness was for Jesus to show that he was the Son of God. Suggest to your students that sometimes when things are difficult in our lives, it's an opportunity for God to get the glory.
3. The sisters were grieving the emotional loss of Lazarus, and each wanted him to be alive. They knew Jesus could heal (verse 27), but they didn't understand what God could do. Jesus had waited, not because he didn't care (verse 5), but probably because Lazarus had already died (verse 14).
4. Let students look over their answers. The word here

for cry is not an uncontrollable crying or wailing, so he wasn't overwhelmed or out of control. However, Jesus cried. No matter the reason, we see Jesus sad and reacting as one who understands (Hebrews 4:15). Discuss with students if we should cry over the things that make Jesus cry.
5. Have students share their descriptions. Some may be gross, and that's okay (just make sure they're appropriate). Build from these to talk about sin, its effect, and how it connects to "grave clothes." If you want, ask students what would've happened if Jesus had simply said, "Come forth" without saying Lazarus' name specifically. Would all the dead in the tomb have come out? Finish by reminding the students that sin is not to bind us, because Jesus has power over sin.

CLOSE

With sensitivity toward any students' current or past grieving, let students know that it's at moments when people pass away that we're reminded how fragile and precious life is. The scene of Jesus standing before the tomb of Lazarus reminds us of his power over death and his offer of eternal life. The unwrapping of the grave clothes reminds us of his desire for us to obey him and be holy as we do his work. His tears reveal his great compassion and love for people. In what ways do your students need to experience Christ's love this week? Wrap up by affirming for your students God's love for them.

MORE

• Mary and Martha are key characters in this story. An interesting extra might be to do a character study on Martha. Have students check out the following verses: Luke 10:38-42; John 11:1, 20-24, 27, 39; and 12:2. What kind of person do you think Martha was? People can criticize Martha, but look at the verses and write down what Martha believed and how she was gifted. How does her personality compare to her sister Mary's? Which do you think you'd most be like?

• For an alternative closing, have students get in groups of eight to 10 and give each group four rolls of toilet paper. Have each group pick a "Lazarus" and wrap that person completely up with the toilet paper. Have students sit down around that person for a few minutes and look at the person while they think of things that keep people (others, friends, even themselves) from being free. Students can name these things out loud as they focus on the person in the "grave clothes." Jesus wants to display his power in their lives by freeing them from what holds them back. Remind them that Jesus didn't take off Lazarus' grave clothes—but others did. Ask students to slowly and quietly (good luck!) take the grave clothes off Lazarus. As they do, mention some ways that they can help free others from what holds them back from experiencing God's forgiveness and freedom.

1. When you think of the word *shepherd*, what pictures come to your mind? Write some words or phrases, or draw a picture.

2. Get with two other people and create a job description for a shepherd. Have each person look up one of the following for help: Genesis 31:38-40; 1 Samuel 17:34-35, 37; and Matthew 15:4-7.

Based on these stories, what was a shepherd supposed to do?

3. On your own, check out John 10:10-11. According to these verses, what does the thief do?

What does Jesus do?

4. Put an "M" on the line below based on how you felt this week.

◀ • ▶

God cares   I don't know
for me   if God cares

5. What would you commit to doing this week to consider how Jesus can be your shepherd? Put a check-mark next to one of the following:

___ Pray for five minutes each morning about that day, asking for God's guidance.
___ Look for ways I can help others who may need to know God loves them.
___ Sit down each night, read John 10:14, and pray.
___ Be alert for ways the thief, Satan, may try to disrupt my relationship with God.
___ Consider if there are any "lions" in my life from whom I need Jesus to protect me.
___ I don't know yet.

THIS WEEK

In some parts of the world, the image of Jesus as the Good Shepherd is so important and meaningful that most churches have a painting up front in their meeting space. This TalkSheet helps students discover what it means that Jesus is the Good Shepherd and lets them discuss ways he can guide them each week.

OPENER

Have everyone clear the floor area and ask for two volunteers. Put one at one end of the room and blindfold them while others put a bunch of small obstacles (books, chairs, etc.) in their way. Tell the blindfolded person they'll have to get to the other end of the room without hitting any obstacles. After their reaction, add that the second person will give them verbal instructions. Tell the others to be quiet as the blindfolded person navigates his or her way to the other side. Now get one more volunteer and set up the same scenario. Once the person is blindfolded, get two more volunteers to give the verbal instructions. However, whisper to one of them that they're to give bad advice and not tell the truth. Tell the blindfolded person to go and, while walking across, listen to these two for instructions. The resulting confusion, the interactions between the three, and the inevitable bump into something will be the desired result.

When finished, get one more volunteer and blindfold him or her. Tell the volunteer to get safely to the other side, but without instructions. Tell them you're going to rearrange the objects on the floor. Act as if you're ready and say "go" again, but at the last minute, ask for another volunteer from the group. Have them come up, stand behind the person, and whisper instructions into the blindfolded person's ears—even steering them a bit with their hands if needed. When finished, ask students to compare the experiences of the blindfolded people. What happened in the second run? Which one was most effective and why? Thank your volunteers and transition to the discussion.

DISCUSSION

1. Are any of your students familiar with raising farm animals? Sheep? Or are all of their images from their readings of the Bible? Have some students share their answers. Do any describe what a shepherd does, or were they mostly about how shepherds looked?

2. The job of a shepherd was difficult and required careful attention and endurance. They provided day and night protection, finding water and pasture. A shepherd had to pay for any lost sheep, an interesting fact in light of Jesus' story in Luke 15:4-6. Work with your students to create a job description on the board, one that would work if you were advertising for an opening.

3. Discuss with your students what it means to live life to the full. In some translations, the word is abundant, which means "a surplus or overflow." What is it to have a surplus of life?

4. What are some reasons people might not think about God's care for them? What are ways God has cared for your students? Give them 20 seconds to silently reflect, and then ask for some answers. Finish by asking people to raise their hands if they have one they're thinking of that's too personal to share.

5. Read John 10:14: "I am the good shepherd; I know my sheep and my sheep know me." Talk to students about what it means to have a relationship with Jesus. He wants to care for us as a shepherd cares for his sheep, but we often see him more like a judge, a faraway God, a big dad, or a nice old man. Jesus wants to be near to us. In fact, he is close and waiting (Revelation 3:20).

CLOSE

Close by talking about Jesus as our guide and our shepherd. How does this work for middle schoolers? Can they really let God guide them, or is it difficult for them to do? Remind them that the sheep's responsibility is to obey the shepherd. Read 1 Peter 2:25: "For you were like sheep going astray, but now you have returned to the Shepherd and Overseer of your souls." Share with students how God has been the overseer of your soul and how that relationship has grown through the years. Remind them that the goal is to get to know the Shepherd, Jesus Christ, and to follow him. You may want to invite students to talk with you after this session if they need to. Pray for your students and their commitments in question #5.

MORE

• **To learn about shepherding before leading this session, read the Wikipedia page (en.wikipedia.org/wiki/Shepherd). Get a heavy wool cloak, a shepherd's staff, a sling, a leather or canvas bag (for food), and a small reed flute (used to calm the sheep) to aid with visuals. Beforehand, put some water in pitchers at one end of a table and some snacks at the other. Have your group stand and "herd" together. You can act as the shepherd and lead them around—first toward the food, then the water, and then back to their spots to rest. You may want someone to read Psalm 23 as you do this. Debrief the experience for any observations they may have.**

• **This is a great session for an evangelistic theme. Sheep are helpless without a shepherd (Matthew 9:36), yet a thief exists who's trying to steal from the flock (John 10:10). Unlike sheep, we can be alert (1 Peter 5:8-9) and resist (James 5:7-8) Satan's influence. Sheep can choose whether to follow the shepherd or not. Read Luke 15:7 and talk about how someone can repent and receive Christ. Talk about the party heaven throws each time someone gives her heart and life to Christ. Close with prayer.**

1. If I lose something, I usually (pick one):

___ Don't worry about it.   ___ Search for it until I find it.

___ Get mad.   ___ I never lose anything.

___ Panic.   ___ Get a new one.

___ Get in trouble.   ___ Oh, I lost the answer.

___ Expect others to find it.

AT THE END OF THE ROAD
The lost son
(Luke 15:11-32)

2. Why do you think some kids run away? Write down two or three reasons.

3. Check out Luke 15:11-17. For what did the son ask the father?

What did he do with what he received (verse 30)?

Where did the son "find" himself?

4. Now read verses 20-24. Match where the father was with what he did.

The father was…	He reacted by…
Gone from home	Running toward the son
Busy with his own life	Not recognizing the son
Looking for his son to come back	Waiting for the son

5. Read verse 32. What's the son's relationship with his dad now?

Write "ME" where you think you are in the box as it describes your relationship with God.

I feel lost.	I need God's embrace.
I know where I am.	God and I are celebrating life together.

From *Middle School TalkSheets: 50 Ready-to-Use Discussions on the Life of Christ* by Terry Linhart. Permission to reproduce this page granted only for use in buyer's youth group. Copyright © 2009 by Youth Specialties. www.youthspecialties.com

THIS WEEK

Running away from home. Sounds tempting sometimes, doesn't it?—especially when we want to get away from rules and get the chance to make our own choices. The story Jesus told of the son who ran away from home involved more than just leaving home—it was a rejection of the father and his love. And yet, at the end of the road, the son returned to find the father waiting at the end of the lane—waiting with loving arms. This is a powerful image of God's unfailing love for people, no matter where they may be in life.

OPENER

Bring in about five items, the more unusual the better, from a local Lost and Found area or from around your house. Ask for six volunteers to compete in a game called Lost and Found Stories. Divide them into pairs and let each pair pick one of the items. Have them make up a 60-second story about how the item was lost. Let them perform their stories and ask the audience which one seemed the most unusual and which the most realistic. Applaud the performers as they sit down, and then have students spend a few minutes sharing moments when *they've* been lost. Have any of their parents ever gotten lost on a trip? How did their parents react when that happened? Discuss with your students what it means to be lost. Are there different examples? If they get stuck, prompt them with ideas like not having a clue in social situations, not understanding homework, or not being sure where they are.

DISCUSSION

1. Read off each one and have students raise their hands for the one they selected. Is there a right answer? How would someone get in trouble for losing something?

2. Ask your students to share some of their answers. Close this question by reminding the students of the serious problems of runaways. Thousands of kids run away each year, and their lives become a nightmare—most often with drug use, prostitution, and a rough life living on the streets.

3. For a son to ask for his portion at this point meant that he thought of his father as though he'd already died—an offense that could result in stoning (Deut. 21:18-21). Ask students how they would've reacted if they were the father. Where was the son when he "found" himself?

4. The father not only was looking for his son, but also he ran toward him despite everything the son had done. Discuss with students how God has run toward us by sending Jesus Christ to save the world from sin and its effect.

5. The father said the son was "found." It was up to the *father* to declare this—he was the father's son and now he was home. And it was a big happy party! Remind students that if they feel lost, God is like the father in the story—waiting to welcome them at any point for any reason.

CLOSE

God is able to forgive, and he saves all who respond—even those who once chose to run away from him. This would be a great time to remind students of God's forgiveness. Jesus talks about once being lost, but now being found, and he illustrates it in the scenes of the son's awareness at the end of the road and the father's welcome. Read Romans 6:23; Acts 3:19; and Romans 10:9-10. Show how repentance is similar to what the lost son says in Luke 15:18-19. Challenge your students to think about their relationships with God, reminding them that you and others are available to talk to after the session.

MORE

• **There are some good video adaptations of the prodigal son story on YouTube.com or GodTube.com. Check them out ahead of time. Start with www.youtube.com/watch?v=Wl29ADCg8X4 or www.youtube.com/watch?v=e-00yOXmm_Y. After you show the clip, ask students what they observed. What does the video show that can be missed in just reading the story?**

• **This session doesn't focus at all on the older son, but if you have time, have students read his story in Luke 15:25-32. How did the elder son think he pleased his dad? What did he expect for his hard work? What did he expect to happen as the logical result of his brother's disobedience?**

• **You may want to spend a few moments teaching your kids about the serious issue of teenage runaways. Do some research online for current statistics and stories. Being a runaway leads to numerous very serious problems. Your group may want to explore ways they can get involved through support or awareness-creating. For more information, check out these groups:**

• **www.education-options.com ("Understanding and Preventing Teenage Runaways")**

• **www.troubledteen.com/teen-troubles/running-away ("Troubled Teen: Running Away—When to Get Your Teen Help")**

• **www.youtube.com/watch?v=ag3cXLFyG2E ("Real Life Teens: Teens and Runaways")**

• ***You Don't Have to Learn Everything the Hard Way* (available at Amazon.com)**

1. Draw a stick figure on the line to show what position on the line best describes your feelings.

◄ • ►

I'm happy   I often think about
with what I have   what I want to buy

2. In each category, write in the items you own that would be the most difficult for you to live without.

Food _____   Clothing _____

Electronics _____   Hobby/Music/Sport _____

Something in your room _____

Something outdoors _____

3. Write down something you got recently (new clothes, toy, electronics, sports item) that made you happy.

4. Read a story that Jesus told in Matthew 19:16-24. Why do you think the man was sad?

5. For each of the following, answer "T" (True) or "F" (False).

_____ A wealthy person thinks about his or her stuff a lot.

_____ A wealthy person has a strong appetite to get more stuff.

_____ The wealthier a person is, the happier the person is.

_____ I'd like to be richer than I am.

_____ People who are richer are better than those who are poor.

_____ I would describe myself as someone who is giving.

6. Proverbs 23:4 says, "Do not wear yourself out to get rich." Paul says in Philippians 4:12, "I have learned the secret of being content in any and every situation." Are there areas of your life where you're really seeking more—and it's almost all you can think about? Write down those areas where you need to learn to be satisfied with what you have.

THIS WEEK

Teens and adults are bombarded with advertising, calling them to get in on the latest trend in fashions, buy the newest gadgets, and to do what everyone else is doing. This TalkSheet gives your middle schoolers a chance to explore the topic of wealth and reflect on the materialistic pressures they face.

OPENER

To start off, it's important to get your students discussing whether they think they're conditioned to recognize and purchase certain brands. Start by showing very short video segments of popular commercials. Play just a small segment and see if your teens instantly recognize them. Or start a common advertising slogan and see if your students can finish it. Get these from TV, Internet, or the newspaper. Divide the room into two teams and see which team gets them first. On the board, write the names of two competing brands and see which one your students prefer and why. Do this for four or five pairs of major brands (soda, clothing, cars, peanut butter, etc.). Why do many people have strong preferences for particular brands? Does advertising really have an influence? Why or why not?

DISCUSSION

1. Draw the line and labels from the TalkSheet on the board and have each student come up and initial the line indicating what they chose on the Talk-Sheet. Use this as a discussion starter for how satisfied students are with their possessions.

2. Ask for some of the items your students wrote down here. Keep this moving—it could start to move slowly. When finished, note any observations you or students have about what the group members value.

3. Do your students feel happier when they get something new, such as new clothes? Explore that with your students. What about it makes them happy? Tell a story of when you really wanted something, got it, and thought you'd be satisfied, only to find yourself wanting more.

4. Show students that the man looked like he was following the commandments, but still lacked God's love for others. Show students that he really didn't love others as he did himself, since he was unwilling to give to the poor.

5. Go through each of these and ask what students answered. People who have "stuff" usually think about it—and our culture wants us to get better and bigger stuff to replace it. Discuss that for a few minutes. It's actually true that the more materialistic a person is, the less happy that person is. Yet it's easy to show respect for a richer person and think she has it all together, while we see a poor person and think the opposite. In this culture, how can middle schoolers learn to be giving? This might be worth kicking around a bit to see how your group can become a giving group. Take on a project so students can give their time and/or money to accomplish something helpful.

6. Discuss with your students what contentment looks like. Does it even seem possible today?

CLOSE

So what *do* we do with the stuff we possess? It may be helpful to talk about what it means to be a steward versus being the owner. What if we committed our stuff to God and let him be the owner? It's easy to lose our way and see our happiness as coming from our possessions—and that's just why the man went away sad. His status and security weren't in God, even though he was religious—it was in his possessions. It's not wrong to be rich, but money and "stuff" aren't to be the focus of our lives. We're to use what we have to bless others through our generosity.

MORE

• **If you have an Internet connection the whole group can see, take students to www.globalrichlist.com and type in $4,000—what a typical high school student could make in a year. Show students where that ranks in the world. Type in $40,000, what a teacher in a local school might make, and show them where that ranks on the world's wealth list. Ask students whether this makes us rich or not.**

• **There are many great resources to help you with projects your group can be plugged into. Youth Specialties has One Life Revolution at www.oneliferevolution. org—or you can get the book *Generation Change* by Zach Hunter to help challenge your students to make a financial difference. Compassion International also offers opportunities to sponsor a child. It's a fantastic challenge for a youth group because it takes a bit of work for middle schoolers to keep it going year-round.**

1. Give a definition of what it means to be fair.

2. Jesus told a story about God's kind of fairness. Read Matthew 20:1-2. How much did these workers agree to make?

NO FAIR!
The workers in the vineyard
(Matthew 20:1-16)

Now, read verse 3. What time did the owner get more workers?

How much money did they agree to work for?

In verses 6 and 7, what time was it and what did the people do?

Now read verses 8-12. What was the problem, according to the first group hired?

Was that fair or not?

3. Why did Jesus tell this story? Check out Matthew 19:27 and pick the one that best explains Peter's concern.

___ I've left everything for your kingdom. I hope to get something in return.
___ How can you give rewards to others when I've been following you for years?
___ You said you'd build your church on me. Who are these other people?
___ Peter has the wrong motives for why he's serving Jesus.

4. Sarah spent most of her life uninterested in the things of God, avoiding going to church. In fact, not only was she involved in all sorts of wild stuff, she was downright mean to her Christian friends. This continued until well past high school. When she was about 25, she had a bad drug overdose at a party and ended up in the hospital. As she breathed her last, she confessed her sin and asked God to forgive her and accept her as his child—which he did, and threw a big party for her in heaven.

Should God have forgiven Sarah?

How do you feel about God "throwing a party" for people who give their lives to Christ in their last minutes?

5. Which of the following best describes what is meant by "the last will be first and the first will be last" in Matthew 20:16?

a. Those who let others go first are better than those at the front of the line.
b. In the end, the line will be reversed and the people at the end will be first.
c. There is no "first" or "last" in God's kingdom—all are equally his children.
d. We need to make sure we're last so we can earn God's approval.

THIS WEEK

A common cry on a playground or at any sporting event is, "That's not fair!" We feel like others get more recognition, attention, opportunities, and benefits than we do, while nothing seems to come our way. In God's economy, grace is given freely. We are never too far from God—his love and attention are equally given to all.

OPENER

Do your students think other people get more breaks than they do? Write the phrase "That's Not Fair!" on the board. Hand out blank cards and have the students write down instances when things happened to them that weren't fair. On the left side of the board, write some prompts such as *brothers/sisters, teachers, coaches, drawings for prizes, classes, work, other families,* and *church.* Have students hand the cards back in to you, then you read the cards aloud, making sure not to mention specific names. Another person can write some of the key phrases on the board. What do you notice about what your group mentioned? Doesn't everyone feel that life has been unfair at times? Is life supposed to be fair? Is God fair?

DISCUSSION

1. Have your students share their definitions. Write some of the key phrases on the board. Do your students equate fairness with goodness? Can someone be fair and not good?

2. Walk through the answers with your students. You may even want to read the story again. What's the main objection of the workers? Were they right to feel that way? Where have you heard people say "That's not fair" recently?

3. What did your students pick as the best explanation? In what ways is Peter saying, "That's not fair"? Peter wants to know what the rewards are for being Jesus' disciple and whether he'll get a greater reward since he's been following Jesus longer and with greater commitment than others.

4. Remind students that everyone can experience God's salvation and love equally. Some don't get more of God's favor than others. This story confronts one of the common errors we make when we think about being a Christian—that we have

to work to earn God's approval. We obey because we're following Christ and he asks us to obey—not to get him to like us more.

5. Work through these and help students think about the implications of each item being true. Discuss reasons why people are so concerned with where they stand "in line." You can take this one deeper, if appropriate, discussing the role our own insecurity plays and our desire to think we're better than someone else.

CLOSE

Read verse 15 aloud and have students consider what it means that God is generous. Ask them to share ways in which God has been generous to them. Can they think of anything? List them on the board, making sure they think about the physical, social, cultural, spiritual, material, and mental areas of life. God's greatest gift was Jesus Christ. There will now be no blame on those who believe in him (Romans 8:1). There are ups and downs in this life, heartaches and joys, tragedies and victories. Tough times will come and sometimes it may not seem fair, but our job is to respond to each moment as God wants us to, trusting him and knowing he's in control.

MORE

• **A contemporary example of people arguing about fairness is fans with referees at sporting events. Why do people argue with referees? What's the purpose? For examples of bad referee calls, see jettingthroughlife. blogspot.com/2006/07/top-10-worst-referee-calls. html. Or, for a classic online video, view www.fliggo. com/video/xKaGWwIL.**

• **It may be helpful to study some of the people in the Bible who went through difficult times, such as Job in Job 1:13-22; 2:7-10; Paul in 2 Corinthians 4:7-11; 11:23-33; and other believers in Hebrews 11:32-40. Another good passage to discuss is James 5:7-11, which encourages patience. It includes verse 9, which says to not "grumble," which also means "grudge not"—or, don't complain, "That's not fair!"**

1. Give a definition of greatness. What does it mean to be great?

BEING GREAT, PART 1
James and John
(Mark 10:35-45)

2. Mark the following as VG (very great), G (great), and NG (not very great):

____ babysitting your younger siblings without getting paid

____ finishing first in a marathon

____ having dinner with the President of the United States

____ getting better grades than your friends do

____ helping out at the homeless shelter

____ being nominated for the scholarship your best friend was hoping to get

____ having a housecleaner to clean up after you

____ making it to nationals with your sports team

____ doing the dishes after supper

____ cleaning the bathroom

3. Read Mark 10:35-45. What do James and John want? Why do they think they deserve this?

What did Jesus say would be required for that to happen?

How did the other disciples respond?

4. Take a look at Philippians 2:5-11. List the steps down that Jesus took to come to earth on the left side and the resulting steps up to the greatness that was given to him on the right side.

_____   _____

_____   _____

_____   _____

<u>Jesus died on the cross and rose from the dead</u>

5. What are two ways people at your school try to be great?

THIS WEEK

Greatness and prestige are highly valued in our society. In their attempts to achieve greatness, most people worry about how they can get ahead, how they can outdo their neighbors, how they can build their resumes, and so on. Jesus had an entirely different approach to greatness. The challenge this week is to lead students to understand true greatness by discussing the model of servanthood left by Christ for us to follow.

OPENER

Begin your discussion time by asking students to get into groups of three and make a list of the top five greatest people that have ever lived. Allow some time for each group to share their lists, and ask them to explain why they chose each person. What qualities made them great? Transition into their definitions from that idea of "great."

DISCUSSION

1. How do your kids define greatness? What would your students like to be great at doing? Do they have a desire to be great? Students may vary in what they think qualifies as greatness. Don't give your definition of greatness at this point in the session.
2. How did your students rate the list of activities? What did they think was the greatest achievement? What was deemed least great? Engage them in conversation about how they decided which of these were great or not.
3. Walk through these answers and try to set the scene of each moment.
4. Jesus took on the attitude of a servant, making himself nothing. Discuss with your students Jesus' divine nature and the nature he took on as a servant. Notice the magnitude of Jesus' greatness in verses 9-11. Can your students give other examples of how Jesus served others?
5. Ask students where greatness comes from. What's the source of greatness? Is it something we do,

something we work to develop, or something we're given? If people see us instead of Christ in us, is that great? Knowing what Jesus values, what steps are your students willing to take toward true greatness and away from how the world may define greatness?

CLOSE

James and John wanted to know how to be great, but Jesus had been showing them all along. As Jesus' disciples, they had the opportunity to observe his character over and over. Jesus constantly taught and modeled servanthood to his disciples, but they missed the classes. Close by discussing the tension between trying to be somebody through worldly greatness and the call to be "empty" so God can fill us and use us to serve others.

MORE
• Another option is to start with the card game President/Scum of the Earth. Rules can be found at www.pagat.com/invented/scum_of_the_earth.html. After playing the game, students can talk about how it feels to be scum and how the president treats the scum. Students who reach the status of president and vice president can also reflect on the way they worked to get to the top (i.e., treating others like scum).
• Check out how loving God and others ties in with servanthood in Galatians 5:13-15; Matthew 22:34-40; and John 13:1-17. It may be beneficial to divide students into teams and assign each a passage to discuss. You may want to give them a question or two to answer as they study. After five minutes, give teams the opportunity to share their observations about love and servanthood with the group—and how this can translate into living love and service to others.

(Thanks to Holly Birkey for this TalkSheet idea)

1. Which of the following skills is something you do well? Put an "X" next to your top three.

___ Cooking   ___ Basketball/volleyball

___ Singing   ___ Gardening

___ Drawing   ___ Band/choir

___ Reading   ___ Text messaging

___ Sleeping   ___ Running/swimming

___ Dancing   ___ Listening

___ Baseball/soccer   ___ Writing

___ Working   ___ Praying

___ Cars/bikes   ___ Studying

___ Video   ___ Other

BEING GREAT, PART 2
The 10 talents
Matthew 25:14-30

2. Write below three to five particular talents, interests, responsibilities, or skills you think you have, or that someone has noticed you have. Put a checkmark next to the ones that define you best—when you're doing them you feel like you're being who you really are.

3. Get with some others around you and read Jesus' story in Matthew 25:14-30. Summarize what happened by filling in the boxes below:

SERVANT	NO. OF BAGS	WHAT THEY DID	MASTER'S RESPONSE	THE RESULT?
First				
Second				
Third				

4. Which of the following best explains why the third servant did what he did?

___ He didn't think the master would return, so he didn't want to give it to a bank and have the talent recognized as belonging to the master—that way he could keep it for himself.

___ He was just lazy and wanted to do the easiest thing with his talent.

___ He wanted to do what was safe so he wouldn't lose the master's talent.

___ He just didn't care what happened to the master's talent.

5. When it comes to the talents I have, which of the following best describes what I do?

❏ **I work hard at my talents, making them as good as they can be.**

❏ **I don't show other people my gifts or talents.**

❏ **I have some gifts and talents, but don't do much with them.**

❏ **I don't know what my gifts and talents are.**

THIS WEEK

This parable focuses on being faithful with our talents and gifts in light of Christ's coming return. Students will explore this teaching of Jesus and plan for faithful actions in their own lives. It's important to make sure this session doesn't emphasize salvation by works or by what we do. The parable before this one in Matthew is about being prepared inwardly, so the two need to be kept in balance.

OPENER

You may want to do this opener before passing out the TalkSheets. Using a melodrama format, read Matthew 25:14-30 while four middle school students act out what you read up front. It's best if you pick students before the meeting and practice this so it'll be funny *and* clear. Pick students who will hold the other students' attention and give the acting some sizzle. It's also important to avoid using the same students who usually do stuff up front—try for diversity and fairness.

After the melodrama, ask what words come to mind that explain what it means to be faithful. List these on the board. Prompt students to think about work, school, sports or music groups, relationships, and their relationship with God. If you don't hear it, make sure to include the word *responsibilities* on the board.

DISCUSSION

1. Students will check a variety of items. Pick three or four and ask, "How many of you put a mark beside _____?" You may want to ask the group to raise their hands to show how they decided they were good at that. Also, it's always fun to ask for "text messaging" as one of the options.
2. Some students might have problems making this list and you may want to discuss the reasons for that. Encourage your students to explore what they can do—to take advantage of different opportunities and not to be scared to see what a possible area of talent or skill is.
3. Draw or project this chart up front and fill it out with your students' comments. Note that there's no ranking here of the three servants. The first two were equally faithful, using their talents to double what the master had given them.
4. All four are various explanations that Bible scholars have proposed. Which one did most of your students select? Walk your students through these four, but have them think of their lists in questions one or two and put those ideas in place of the word "talent."

How do these help us think about what we're to do with our talents and gifts?
5. Remind students that this story describes being great as being faithful with what God has given to us—our gifts, talents, and opportunities. Don't have students share their answers, but talk through this list of options with them and finish by encouraging them to develop the abilities that God has given them.

CLOSE

This session has the possibility to make some kids feel inferior, as if they have no talents. You don't want to let that happen, so keep it encouraging and upbeat. Tell students that God gave us our gifts and talents, so he's the owner (we're not to keep them to ourselves), and he wants us to invest (develop) them so he can use them to grow his kingdom. In this way we're being great *for God* so that every time we serve, play music, play sports, study, create, organize, lead, follow, give, teach, encourage, repair things, or any other activity that takes talent or skill, we do it to the best of our ability so that God gets the glory (1 Corinthians 10:31). Knowing that it comes from God and that we're doing it for God can really take the pressure off and the ego out of our service. Close with a short story from your life—or have another adult share one—that gives an example of developing a talent or skill that God has given.

MORE

• **The parable of the talents is focused on the outward spiritual life—being faithful through working for God. The parable before this in Matthew of the ten bridesmaids, focused on the faithfulness of being prepared in our inward spiritual life. Which is easier to do: Think of the Christian life as something we do outwardly, or something within?**

• **This may be a good session to have someone come in and talk with your students about spiritual gifts. Some would say it's difficult for a middle schooler to know what his or her gifts and talents are—a concern that has some validity. So don't push students, but rather, educate them about spiritual gifts from these passages: Romans 12:6-8; 1 Corinthians 12:4-30; Ephesians 4:7-12; and 1 Peter 4:10. Schooling can often label students and reinforce feelings of inferiority in some and self-dependence in others, even at the middle school level. Remind students that the gifts and talents we're given are not ours and that God is expecting us to use what he has given to the best of our ability, not hide in fear.**

1. When was the first time you remember hearing about Jesus Christ?

When you were little, did you have any funny thoughts about God? If so, what were they?

2. Check out Matthew 21:1-11. Write down what the people said as Jesus entered the city.

3. Turn to the prophecy in Zechariah 9:9 and write down as many ways as you can see that it connects to Jesus' entrance.

4. The crowd at Jesus' entrance shouted "Hosanna," while the crowd at Jesus' trial a few days later (Matthew 27:20-23) shouted, "Crucify him!" The opinion of the city had turned on Jesus. Which of the following best explains why in your opinion?

_____ The religious leaders stirred up the crowd, and the people just followed along.

_____ The people thought Jesus would overthrow the Roman government.

_____ It was Satan's influence on the people of the crowd.

_____ This was a different group of people from those who welcomed Jesus into Jerusalem.

5. Jesus went to Jerusalem for a specific purpose. In Matthew 20:17-19, Jesus announced, "We are going up to Jerusalem, and the Son of Man will be delivered over to the chief priests and the teachers of the law. They will condemn him to death and will hand him over to the Gentiles to be mocked and flogged and crucified. On the third day he will be raised to life!" Read that and write down how it makes you feel.

THIS WEEK

At the end of Jesus' public ministry, he arrived like a king in Jerusalem, an entrance that began a series of God-orchestrated events leading to his death and resurrection. This TalkSheet gives students the opportunity to understand the significance of Jesus' arrival and to reflect on how he has come into their lives.

OPENER

Get five volunteers from your group and have them come up front. In a funny talk-show format, do a short, fun interview with each one, asking how each one enters a room at school, at a youth group party, or at home. Do they think about their entrances? Does anyone in your group think about how they want to enter a room? Have the five students leave the room, telling them you want them to work on making a grand entrance. Introduce them one by one and have them enter the room with style, as if they were stars. After each one makes his or her entrance, have students share what they liked about those entrances.

Clap for your volunteers as they sit down, and ask students if they can think of any dramatic run in entrances by heroes in movies. You may want to think of some examples beforehand too. As students give their own examples, write them down on a whiteboard up front. Get a good list and then ask students why those scenes are so easy to remember. How do these entrances make people feel?

Tell students you're going to read about a triumphant entry in the Bible. Like most movies, this arrival marked a serious change in the storyline, one that ultimately affected the ending of the story. Ask for a volunteer student with a good voice to stand up and read Matthew 21:1-11.

DISCUSSION

1. Have students volunteer to share their early thoughts of God. Do some online searches for funny things kids say about God and read the best to your students.
2. When Jesus came down the Mount of Olives across the Kidron Valley, he was in plain view of the Roman soldiers along the walls of Jerusalem. As the crowd surged around him, waving palm branches, the word spread. Jesus made a public entrance and the religious leaders were forced to act (John 12:19). Jesus knew the cross was ahead and this entrance was his declaration that he had come to Jerusalem. The shouts of "Hosanna" meant "Save us, we pray" and are taken from Psalm 118:25-26.
3. Remind students of the fact that the fulfillment of Old Testament prophecies in Jesus' life is very important (see TalkSheet #1 for more). Walk students through how each phrase was fulfilled at Jesus' entrance.
4. Though no one really knows whether the two crowds were comprised of the same people, the people of Jerusalem in that time expected the Messiah to have an earthly kingdom, centered in Jerusalem. They expected Jesus to deliver them from Roman rule, the invaders occupying the land and oppressing them. Jesus, however, preached about an eternal kingdom, and his focus was on saving people from their sins so they could be welcomed into that kingdom. You may want to discuss ways we expect Jesus to fix our problems.
5. Help students think of ways that Jesus has made an arrival into their lives. Because of this arrival into Jerusalem and his death and resurrection, Jesus can now live within us and be our guide through his Spirit. How have we responded to Jesus? Have we said "Hosanna"? Are we asking, "Who is this?" It's okay to ask who Jesus is as long as we're interested in seeking the answer. You may want to share the story of how you gave your life to Christ here.

CLOSE

Jesus' arrival in Jerusalem started a chain of God-orchestrated events that has changed the world. He arrived as a king to those who knew him, was beaten, ridiculed, and killed for the sins of the world, rose from the dead, and left as Lord and Savior of the entire earth. Explain that God seeks to arrive in each of our lives and wants to be our Lord and Savior. Find a good song that invites listeners to follow Christ or connects to the shouts of "Hosanna!" and play it. Make sure to have the lyrics up front or on handouts for students to follow.

MORE

• **Get three poster boards and write each of the three phrases people say in verse 9 at the top of each one. Put them up around the room and briefly set the context for each one. Encourage students to come up and write an additional praise underneath each one. What would *they* say out loud as Jesus came into *their* city? If you want, you can also add the question from verse 10 on a poster board and have students write their answers under each one. For larger groups, you'll need more than three poster boards. Play some good music as students do this one!**

• **This session could easily be turned into a full-out gospel presentation. As you discuss the differences between knowing Jesus and knowing *of* him, challenge the students with the question, "Do you really know Jesus personally, or have you only heard about him?" Verses to take them through could include John 1:12; 5:24; Romans 3:23; 5:8; 6:23; and Titus 3:5. Give students a chance to respond. This is a great illustration to challenge students who have been to church their entire lives, but have never accepted Jesus as Lord.**

(Thanks to Tom Carpenter for this TalkSheet idea)

1. If you knew you were going to be able to eat a "last supper" at the end of your life, what would you choose to eat?

THE LAST SUPPER
Jesus prepares the
disciples for his death
(Matthew 26:17-30)

2. When your family wants to celebrate over a meal, what do they do?

    Order carryout
    Eat pizza
    Go to a nice restaurant
    Watch a movie and eat snacks
    Prepare a big meal at home
    Invite friends over

3. Check out Matthew 26:17-18 and Mark 12:12-15. What kinds of preparations did Jesus make for the last meal with his disciples?

4. Read Matthew 26:20-25. Why did the disciples ask Jesus if it would be they who would betray him?

    ___ They knew they had doubts.   ___ They were being polite.

    ___ They didn't want to disappoint the Master.   ___ They were scared of the Romans.

    ___ They believed, but were distressed.   ___ They were questioning themselves.

5. Read Matthew 26:26-27. What does the bread represent?

Read verses 27-28. What does the wine represent—and what does it provide?

Read verse 29. What do you think Jesus means by this?

Read verse 30. If you were there and chose to sing one meaningful song or hymn at the last supper with Jesus, what song would you have chosen and why?

THIS WEEK

As Jesus neared his death and resurrection, he gathered his disciples together for an intimate time to celebrate the Passover. Through the symbols of the bread and the cup, Jesus instructed them to remember what he was about to do. These symbols and this meal, known as the Lord's Supper, Communion, or the Eucharist, have become one of the most important sacraments of the church today, a reminder of the central belief of Christianity. This TalkSheet gives ample opportunity for you to discuss various aspects of this key church practice with your students.

OPENER

Do your students remember the first time they watched others taking communion? Did they understand what it was about at the time? In what ways has their understanding grown over the years? You may want to write some of the responses from this question on the board. Your students will have a wide range of awareness about communion. What was the experience like for your students when they took communion for the first time?

DISCUSSION

1. Have students share their last meal ideas. Transition by talking about the role that eating a meal plays in your culture. Is it important to their family? To their church? Do their families regularly eat together? Eating a regular meal together (first daily, in Acts 2:42, then later it was done weekly) was a regular practice of the early church.

2. Do your students have family conversation at meals, or are meals just for eating? Ask students if they have special meals for birthdays, Christmas, or Easter. What are they like? Do any of your students have special symbols or traditions at these meals? Are they connected to religious or ethnic traditions?

3. Let students share what they found. Jesus evidently made some decisions and arranged for this special meal. The procedures for how to prepare the Passover were known by all, with specific timing for the sacrifice of the lamb. Jesus instructs Peter and John to prepare the meal, which involved obtaining the food and setting the room. For more, see Exodus 12:3, 6, and 14-17.

4. Each of the disciples, except Judas, calls Jesus "Lord", demonstrating their faith. Judas refers to Jesus as Rabbi, a more formal name for a disciple to call a master. None of the disciples immediately assumed Judas was going to betray Jesus—they first asked if it were any of them!

5. Go over the answers for this question. Read Paul's interpretation in 1 Corinthians 11:23-26. Ask students how Matthew 26:29 shows that Jesus is already looking into the future and past his coming death and resurrection. Read 1 Corinthians 15:20-25. What has Christ done that gives him power? Ask students to share what song or hymn they would've chosen to sing if they were leaving this last supper.

CLOSE

You, or a pastor, can conduct a short communion service at the end of your program if you have the time to do it well. If not, you can focus on the idea of remembrance. When your students want to remind themselves of God, who God is, and what God has done, what do they do? Do they have symbols or activities that are particularly helpful for remembering? Remind students that there's a danger when the symbol becomes more important that the One it reminds them of. Tell students you're going to do what the disciples did on that night—sing a hymn and then leave. Select a song ahead of time, or pick one of the songs mentioned by the students, and sing it as a group without accompaniment. If it fits, consider making this dismissal more reflective by having the students either singing as they leave, reflecting on what Jesus has done for them, or leaving in near silence as the 11 disciples might have done that evening after the Passover meal.

MORE

• For more Scripture about the Lord's Supper, see Paul's interpretation in 1 Corinthians 11:23-26. The symbol of the bread usually stood for God's blessing and provision (Matthew 14:9 and 15:36). The cup was the third cup of the Passover, a cup of thanksgiving and blessing (1 Corinthians 10:16). What blessing should we be thankful for when we take communion? The phrase "blood of the new covenant" was prophesied in Jeremiah 31:31-34, the passage known as the "new covenant."

• If applicable, the opening time would be a great place to hand out copies of your church's (or information from various churches) understanding of communion.

• Some resources online explain what's involved with a Passover meal. Some of the symbolism of the Passover was used by Jesus with his disciples. You can use parts of an online 40-minute video, "Christ in the Passover," found at video.google.com/videoplay?docid=5272606 142394767394 or you can buy it at store.jewsforjesus. org/ppp/product.php?prodid=4.

1. Finish this sentence: When my mom or dad asks me to help around the house, I _____

_____.

What's the messiest job or chore you've ever done?

What was the most difficult job or chore you ever did?

What job around the house do you hate?

THIS JOB STINKS!
Jesus models how to serve
(John 13:1-17)

2. Read John 13:1-5. What do you think verse 3 means?

3. Read verses 6-10. Which of the following best explains Peter's reaction?

Peter didn't understand what Jesus was doing and was telling a joke.

Peter was embarrassed that Jesus had to perform this servant's task.

Peter wanted to have Jesus' complete healing, not just the ceremonial washing of only his feet.

Peter didn't want Jesus to wash his feet, so he tried to act uncomfortable to get Jesus to quit.

Peter needed a bath anyway, so he was making light of that fact.

4. Read what Jesus said in verses 13-17. Rewrite it into a single sentence:

5. If you were a teacher and had to give yourself a grade on your willingness to serve others, what grade would you get? Explain your reasons.

Write down the name of someone you think God may want you to serve this week. What can you do to help that person in a way that means a lot?

THIS WEEK

A symbolic moment of Jesus' intentional modeling for his disciples (and us!) was the scene where he performed one of the most unskilled acts of service of that time—washing the feet of others. When the disciples were not willing to serve others, the great Teacher willingly performed the courtesy and instructed those who could hear to do the same. The challenge remains for us to serve in ways that confront our pride.

OPENER

Beforehand, find 12 dirty jobs (visit the Web site of the television show *Dirty Jobs* for some ideas) and make six either/or pairs that will provide a difficult decision of which job a middle schooler would prefer. Find 10 or 12 pictures of various feet online and create a computer slideshow. Show it behind you as you lead the opening (or the whole session!). Are there chores, jobs, or duties they don't enjoy doing? Tell students you're going to play Would You Rather. Ask them to stand. Announce each pair of jobs and have students choose which one they'd rather do by moving to one side of the room or the other. Get a few responses from students as to why they made their choice. Repeat this for each pair and have students sit down.

DISCUSSION

1. Quickly have students announce their answer to the first sentence. Keep things popping along and try to get most, if not all, of the students to answer. It's a safe one. For the next questions, find the messiest and feel free to follow it up. Do your students enjoy or stay away from messy and difficult jobs?

2. The washing of feet was a common courtesy of the day. Everyone wore sandals or no shoes, and the washing of feet upon entering a home was a way to cleanse feet from the dirt, sand, and sweat so that the eating area could be kept clean. Why did the disciples choose not to wash the others' feet? Jesus stated aloud who he is, and it's from this strength that he was able to serve in a "low" capacity. Our insecurity and concern over what others think about us comes from pride—and that keeps us from being able to give ourselves away for the sake of others. Discuss this with your students to make sure they understand this key point.

3. Have students talk about their answers. How does Peter's personality play a role in how he acted? Do you think the disciples understood what Jesus was saying? You may want to read what Peter wrote later in 1 Peter 5:5-6. Do you think Peter learned his lesson eventually?

4. Ask willing students to share their sentences. What is the significance of these verses? How does your church do at fulfilling these? What would change if you and your students intentionally put this into practice on a regular basis in your group?

5. Remind students that we're often like the disciples—unwilling to serve. Our own sinful pride, selfishness, and concern about what others think of us keep us from reflecting Christ in our service.

CLOSE

Beforehand, prepare well-designed slips of paper with this phrase written on it to hand out to students to take with them as a theme for the week. Write this goal of spiritual formation (from Robert Mulholland's book *Invitation to a Journey*) on the board: "Conform to the image of Christ for the sake of others." Talk through what it means to conform to the image of Christ, and remind them that we do so for others' sake. Encourage them to be alert for ways they're reflecting the character of Jesus in how they act toward others.

MORE

• **If you've never performed a footwashing service, this would be a great moment to do so with your students. Divide the group by gender, boys on one side and girls on the other, so that boys are washing boys' feet and so forth. Play a series of worshipful songs in the background and have a basin of water and a towel by each chair. Each student will wash the feet of the person next to him or her. Check online for helpful Web sites—this is an important and regular service in some denominations.**

• **A subtle aspect of this story and others is how competitive the disciples were with each other. No one wanted to wash the feet of the others, and some fought over who would be greater in heaven than the others (Luke 22:24-30). With your students, list ways people compete with each other at school, with friends, and… at church?! Two passages by Paul (1 Corinthians 9:24-27; 2 Timothy 2:4-7) talk about competition, but not with others. Paul encourages us to compete with different opponents than each other. Have students look up these verses and discuss where our competitive natures are to be focused.**

1. Which of the following have the strongest connection? Check up to three.

❏ Electric fan and power plant
❏ Two close friends
❏ Glue and pieces of paper
❏ Mother and her child
❏ Tree and soil
❏ Person's arm and shoulder
❏ Two people on cell phones
❏ Branch and its vine
❏ Two Red Sox baseball fans
❏ St. Louis and New Orleans

THE TRUE VINE
Being connected to Jesus
(John 15:1-11)

2. What's your favorite fruit to eat?

How did you learn to like that fruit?

3. Read John 15: 1-6. How does a branch bear fruit?

How does Jesus say you can bear fruit?

What is the fruit?

4. Read the following verses and write next to each one how Jesus says that we are to remain in him:

John 6:56—

John 8:31—

John 15:9-10—

5. Look at these fruitful qualities from Galatians 5:22-23 listed below. Put a check next to the ones that you have seen in yourself. Circle the ones that you would like to have more of in your life.

Love ____   Joy ____   Peace ____

Patience ____   Kindness ____   Goodness ____

Self-control ____   Faith ____   Gentleness ____

THIS WEEK

It's common to hear Christian kids in middle school talk about their personal relationship with Jesus. This has different meanings for different people, so this TalkSheet explores how Jesus views his relationship with us. Not only does Jesus provide a great visual example for the disciples, but he also reminds them of a function of the relationship—to be spiritually fruitful, living a godly life.

OPENER

Divide the students into equal-sized groups of no more than eight per group. Tell them they're going to make a short commercial for a fruit. Each group is to try to give the most convincing explanation about why their fruit is the best. Use apples, bananas, grapes, oranges, raspberries—and give one group tomatoes just for fun. Give students a few minutes to make up their commercials, then have the groups perform. Compliment each group and poll students on which commercial they found the most convincing and why. Did the tomato group convince anyone that a tomato is actually a fruit? As students move back to their places, see if any of them can tell you what's involved in the fruit-growing process.

DISCUSSION

1. Ask students to share what they selected and why. You may have to explain how some pairs are connected (for example, St. Louis and New Orleans share a major river, and jazz). Pay attention to the criteria that students used or didn't use to make their selections. What choices didn't get any marks?

2. Let students share their favorite fruits. Keep track of the most popular choices. Did they love fruits from the beginning, or did they learn to like them? Ask students the most unusual fruit they've ever eaten.

3. Remind students that a branch can only bear fruit if it remains connected to the vine. The power and growth of the branch comes not from itself, but from the vine. Discuss students' answers with them—the idea of fruit developing can mean other people coming to faith in Christ (Romans 1:13), our own growth in obeying God (Romans 6:22), and the fruit of the Holy Spirit (Galatians 5:22-23).

4. Let students share what they found. Tell them that to "remain" is not a one-time event, but a continual connectedness in which Christ is the source and

power of our lives. To remain means we accept Jesus as our Savior and continually follow him through obedience and studying his Word. What is the connection, the bond, between Jesus and his followers? Read Romans 8:38-39 and 1 Corinthians 6:19-20 for more.

5. List the fruits of the Spirit (Galatians 5:22-23) on the board. Ask students to think about these fruits in their lives. Are they more loving than they were a year ago? More joyful? Peaceful? And so on. What do they need to do now for the items they circled? Close by reminding them that their relationship with God serves as the source of all spiritual fruit in our lives. Our responsibility is to remain connected and live godly lives—the Holy Spirit produces the fruit in us as we follow Jesus.

CLOSE

Focus on the fruit. Who produces the fruit in our lives? Discuss with students how the fruit in our lives tells our friends and others we know who God is. In what settings is it most difficult to reflect who God is? At home? When we're alone? Talk about the role of our character as an example—the times we're alone or with our family are often the moments the weak areas of our character come out. Pray for your students that they'll have a fruitful character as they remain connected to Jesus.

MORE

• As a visual extra, you may want to have bowls of fruit sitting around the room as students show up. Those listening to Jesus understood what the imagery of the vine meant to Israel, God's people (Isaiah 5:7; Jeremiah 6:9; Hosea 10:1). Jesus uses that image to claim his role as the Messiah, the One who is God in flesh, the true vine. Consequently, he has the power and position to be the center and source of the work in the kingdom of God.

• There is a balance to this topic. God produces the fruit, but we're to do our part as well. To explore this last part more, have students read 1 Corinthians 3:9: "For we are God's co-workers; you are God's field, God's building." Review with students what it means to be a "co-worker" with God. For some Old Testament examples that we have a job to do, check out and discuss Psalm 78:72 and Proverbs 21:31.

1. Do you know of people who regularly pray for you? Write down their names below.

Besides yourself, whom have you prayed for in the last week or so, and what was it about?

2. Read John 17:1-5. Looking at verse 5, what is Jesus focusing on here?

3. Jesus prays for his disciples in verses 13-19. Rewrite each of the following in your own words.

They may have the full measure of joy within them—

They are in the world, but not of the world—

4. Jesus prays for you in his prayer. Look at verses 20-24 to see what he prayed about for you and then circle the letters of any ideas below that he focused on.

       a. That you will have unity and harmony with other Christians.

       b. That your harmony with others would be in unity with Christ and God's purposes.

       c. That others will know God's love because of your love for others.

       d. That you will someday see Jesus in his glory in heaven.

5. What does *unity* mean? Write down as many words, phrases, or examples as you can that help explain it to other middle school students.

What was Jesus praying for when he prayed for unity?

      ❑ It was a hostile world then, and the believers would need to be unified.

      ❑ He knew that the biggest testimony of a church is its love for others.

      ❑ Our selfish natures come out first in our relationships.

      ❑ Unity with God. It's the source for harmony with others.

THIS WEEK

A few hours before his arrest, Jesus paused and prayed to the Father similar to the way a priest would've prayed for those in his care. Other Bible passages on prayer get more attention, but this high priestly prayer is a fascinating glimpse into Jesus' prayer life and the important issues he brought before God, the Father. Jesus also prayed for future believers—which includes you and your students—and for their unity. This and other themes of Jesus' prayer serve as the focus of this TalkSheet discussion.

OPENER

Before this meeting, find some written prayers and references to prayer from magazines, newspapers, the Internet, and your church. Print a collection of prayers that show a range of approaches and different ways of thinking about prayer. Have students team up with others around them, and then pass these papers out so that each group has at least two prayers to read. Have your students read through the prayers. After a few minutes, ask: To whom is the prayer written? What's the focus of the prayer? What's the benefit to writing out a prayer? What do your students think about written prayers—are they authentic when read, or is it better to just pray what comes to your heart?

DISCUSSION

1. Have some students share what they wrote about who prays for whom. How do they know who's praying for them? Does it matter if people pray for us? For whom are your students regularly praying? Why did they choose those people? Spend a few moments here talking with your middle schoolers about their prayer lives.

2. This is an opportunity to teach students that Jesus, as God, had always existed and that he wasn't created when he came to earth as a baby. In verse 4, Jesus knew that the cross was just ahead and that this would bring glory to God, the Father. He looked forward to having his glory back and not being confined to human form. He later prayed that we would see his glory (verse 24). Read more about the preexistence of Jesus in Colossians 1:15-17 and make sure your students know what it means that Jesus existed "before all things."

3. Get some rewrites your students want to share. You may want to write one or two rewrites as well. How can someone be full of joy when it seems like the world is against him?

4. All these are present in Jesus' prayer. Unity as a goal exists because of what Christ has done to extend forgiveness to us, not to draw attention to our churches or ourselves. The goal of our love is for people to understand who God is (Matthew 5:16). How has the unity within your group fared during the last month? What would your students do to promote unity and love among those in your group? What's significant about the fact that Jesus prayed for each one of us?

5. Often, people's two biggest objections to church are: a) It's boring, and b) The people there aren't very nice and don't get along. Discuss students' answers to these questions. Finish by asking a summary question, "What does Jesus' prayer tell us about what we should focus on in our prayers?"

CLOSE

Tell your group that you're going to work on a group prayer. If we were to create the *ultimate* prayer for our group, what would it include? Take ideas from your students and write them on the board. What should we be praying for in a prayer that will last a long time? After you have done this for about four or five minutes, arrange students' ideas in a format that resembles: 1) praying about who God is, 2) praying about who God wants us be, and 3) praying for God's help in doing that. Have someone type the prayer, and distribute it as your group's prayer at your next gathering or via email.

MORE

• **The words *glory* and *glorify* are prominent in this prayer. For further study, students can note each time the word is used in the chapter and its usage. You may want to have students look up Exodus 29:42-43 and 33:18-23; John 1:14 and 12:23; and 2 Peter 1:16-18. Have students read John 14:23-24 and 17:24-26. What do these verses tell us about God's glory? What difference does it make for Christians to be aware of the presence of God's glory in their lives?**

• **You may want to spend some time talking about prayer with your students. Encourage them to invest in their prayer lives. Have them journal each night for one week about their prayers from that day, keeping track of what they pray about and when. Ask students what they expected to discover. What percentage of their prayers were about personal wants? What would happen if students wrote out their prayers before praying them? You may want to establish a Web site where students can post four-sentence prayers on a discussion board. This can promote unity in prayer among your students during the week.**

1. Get with two or three others around you. Which of the people in your group would make the best judge? Lawyer? Convict?

UNJUSTLY ACCUSED
The arrest and trial of Jesus
(Luke 22:47-23:5)

2. Still in your groups, complete the following: The events of Jesus' arrest and sentencing are listed in the probable order of how they happened. To the right of each item, put the letter of the passage that describes that event.

Jesus betrayed by Judas and arrested. _____

A. Matthew 27:27-31

Jesus tried by the Sanhedrin at night. _____

B. Mark 15:15

Jesus beaten by the religious guards. _____

C. John 18:1-8

Jesus before Pilate at daybreak. _____

D. John 19:4-16

Jesus before Herod. _____

E. Matthew 26:59-66

Jesus before Pilate again—and condemned. _____

F. Matthew 27:11-20

Jesus flogged. _____

G. Luke 22:63-65

Roman soldiers mock and beat Jesus. _____

H. Luke 23:8-12

3. Put an "X" next to the events above that were new to you—events you didn't know happened. Write down any reactions you have to what you have read:

4. Which of the following best describes your feelings when you think about Jesus' trial?

_____ I get angry at the way they treated Jesus.

_____ It makes me sad that he had to go through that.

_____ I realize how serious sin is to God.

_____ I know how much God loves me and wants me to live for him.

_____ I want to share the story of what Jesus has done with others.

THIS WEEK
This TalkSheet acquaints students with the events leading up to Christ's crucifixion.

OPENER
Record an episode from one of the many television programs that feature a judge in a court room (like *Judge Judy*). Find an appropriate three-to-four-minute section that's entertaining and funny. You'll also want to know the cue on the recording for the judge's verdict so you'll be able to quickly get there. Tell students what the charges are and show the video clip. Discuss what your students think the verdict will be, getting everyone's vote, and then show the judge's verdict. Transition by asking students if this was a fair trial or not. How was this a realistic courtroom—or not?

DISCUSSION
1. Who would make good judges in each student group? Lawyers? Convicts? What reasons did your groups use to determine who would be best in each group?
2. Go through and figure out the answers yourself so you can make sure everyone gets them correct. This is the main part of the TalkSheet—to expose students to the events of Jesus' arrest and trial. So don't go too quickly. Point out key quotes or moments from each scene and share them as you walk through this. The arrest and trial process broke a number of Jewish laws (arrested at night, taken to the home of a religious leader, tried at night, and convicted on the same day). Why would the religious leaders break so many of their own laws?
3. Ask willing students to share what they wrote. Read Luke 22:39-46. Show how Jesus knew what was to come and agonized in prayer beforehand. Discuss Jesus' obedience to the Father and what it must have been like for the Creator (Colossians 1:16) to have his creation (people) reject and abuse him.
4. From the beginning (Genesis 3:15) and throughout the prophecies of the Old Testament, this moment had been predicted—the moment when the Messiah would come and be the sacrifice for the sins of men and women. How should we respond to this message of what Christ has done? What do the words of Matthew 16:24-25 ("Whoever wants to be my disciple must deny themselves and take up their cross and follow me. For whoever wants to save their life will lose it, but whoever loses their life for me will find it") challenge us to do?

CLOSE
Point out that it can be easy to overlook the great pain and humiliation that Jesus endured before he was crucified. Remind your students that Jesus said the world would also hate his followers (Matthew 10:22 and John 15:18-19). Ask students if they ever think about the fact that many in the world will continue to reject Christ and hate those who follow him. Jesus, however, took this one step further and said that we're to do good to those who hate us (Luke 6:22). Jesus' example through all of this showed his focus on the eternal kingdom, not the temporary one of the Roman government. You may want to find a song or great hymn that focuses on Jesus' suffering and play it. Provide printed lyrics so students can follow along.

MORE
• **For further Bible study, have students focus on the disciples in this story. What was their reaction (Mark 14:50)? Why did they disappear? What did Peter do in the garden (John 18:10) and later in the priest's courtyard (Luke 22:54-62; John 18:15-18, 25-27)? Was it dangerous for Peter to have followed Jesus so closely at this point? What do your students think Pilate thought about Jesus (Matthew 27:11-26; John 18:28-19:16)?**
• **A peripheral topic is the persecution Christians are currently enduring. Find resources at www.missionre-sources.com/persecuted.html and visit the Voice of the Martyrs' Web site at www.persecution.com.**

1. **Which of the following best shows what reconciliation means?**

❏ Two friends make up after a week of being mad.

❏ A runaway comes back and is forgiven and welcomed.

❏ An accountant figures out how much money is in the bank.

❏ A person enjoys the outdoors and feels at home in the woods.

❏ A judge forgives someone because someone else went to jail for them.

THE ULTIMATE SACRIFICE
The death of Jesus on the cross
(Matthew 27:27-58)

2. **Write down what comes into your mind when someone talks about Jesus' death on the cross.**

3. **When Jesus was crucified, what did each of these people do?**

Governor's soldiers (Matthew 27:27-31):

Simon of Cyrene (Matthew 27:32):

The priests, teachers, and elders (Matthew 27:41):

The centurion (Matthew 27:54):

The two criminals (Luke 23:39-41):

Roman soldiers (John 19:23, 24 and 32-34):

4. **Read each of the following phrases Jesus said on the cross. Circle the one you think best explains what Jesus was doing. Put a "Q" next to any you have questions about.**

"Father, forgive them, for they do not know what they are doing." (Luke 23:34)

"My God, my God, why have you forsaken me?" (Matthew 27:46)

"Father, into your hands I commit my spirit." (Luke 23:46)

"It is finished." (John 19:30)

5. **When Jesus died, the large curtain that separated people from God's presence ripped from top to bottom (Matthew 27:51). If you'd been there and seen the curtain tear, what would you have thought or done?**

THIS WEEK

No matter what the denomination or tradition, the central beliefs of the Christian faith are built on the death and resurrection of Jesus Christ. Crosses are common jewelry items, yet it's quite possible that many of your middle schoolers haven't read that Bible story. This TalkSheet exposes students to the events of Jesus' death, reminds them of why Jesus died, and shows what has been gained through his sacrifice for their sins.

OPENER

Option A - If appropriate for your group (preview it!), show the crucifixion scenes from either *The Gospel of John* or *Jesus of Nazareth*. Following the movie, lead a quick discussion about what your students noticed in the movie. If they're slow to answer, mention the various people or scenes in order and have students share observations.

Option B - If you can't show the movie, ask students to remember a famous person who died suddenly. Have them share as many as they can remember. If they have difficulty, prompt them to think about presidents, movie stars, famous musicians, and sports athletes. How did people react to the news? Ask students which of these will be remembered the longest and why. This would be a great moment to share your own story about how you were affected by someone famous passing away.

Transition by telling students that Jesus' life and death have had a significant impact on people throughout history. The story of his death is recorded in all four Gospels. Tell students that Jesus Christ was our substitute, offering himself as a sacrifice in our place, so that we could have forgiveness of sins and a right relationship with God. This effect of this work is called atonement. Have someone read 1 John 2:2.

DISCUSSION

1. Tell students that atonement in the New Testament means "reconciliation" (Romans 5:11). Which of the possible answers focus on reconciliation? Are all of them possible answers? Write the word "redeem" on the board and ask students to help you create a definition. Show your kids that the death of Christ allows people to have a true relationship with God (reconciliation)—they can be forgiven (redeemed) since Jesus died in their place.
2. So what do your kids think about when they think about Christ's death? This is a great chance to see what your kids know and how they feel about the topic.
3. Walk your students through this exercise. It's designed to expose students to different people. You may want to have students consider each person's perspective on the events. For instance, why did the governor's soldiers make fun of Jesus after he'd just been severely beaten?

The word used for the centurion means to "keep on glorifying," so it's possible he changed his beliefs about Jesus.

4. You'll want to review these so you know them and what they mean. Which do your students have questions about? Even as Jesus endured brutality, ridicule, and rejection, he forgave those who beat and mocked him, loving them as their Creator. Jesus sensed a separation from the Father and cried out, quoting Psalm 22:1. Jesus was in full control of when he would give up his life—it wasn't taken from him (John 10:17-18). When it was done, Jesus knew the ransom (Mark 10:45) had been paid in full, and death had been defeated.
5. The curtain reminded people of the holiness of God and their own unrighteous nature. They would never be holy enough to be in God's presence, and the high priest could only go in once a year. God's presence was no longer in the temple—God could now live in men and women because they had forgiveness of sins. Read Hebrews 10:19-20 and ask students to share their opinions of what it would be like to have been there.

CLOSE

Have students look up Isaiah 53:7-9 and follow along as you read it out loud. Ask students to share how the various statements from these verses were true from what they discovered in this session. After a few minutes of discussion, have students close their eyes for some reflection. Remind them of God's immense love for his people and that, though we were the ones who sinned against him, he sent his son Jesus to die in our place. That's an incredible act that is very difficult for us to comprehend. But the curtain has been torn and now we have access to God—he hears our prayers! Read Isaiah 53:7-9 again and close with prayer.

MORE

• For more Bible study, have students turn to Titus 3:4-7. Why did God choose to save us? According to this passage, how does God save us? Check out Luke 23:39-43 and discuss the story of the two thieves crucified on either side of Christ. What did each believe about Christ?

• Write John 15:12-13 on the board: "My command is this: Love each other as I have loved you. Greater love has no one than this: to lay down one's life for one's friends." Christ is the ultimate model of the principle of what it means to be Christian—that we love others by laying down our lives. When is that the easiest to do? The most difficult? Is it hard to lay down your life at home for your siblings? If we went to your friends and asked how well you do at this, what might they say? Help your students develop steps that they can put in place for the next week to help them grow in their Christlikeness in this area.

1. Do you think UFOs exist? Why or why not?

2. What would it take for you to believe that UFOs exist? Rank the following forms of proof from least convincing (1) to most convincing (6).

___ More than three people saw it at different times.

___ I read about it in the newspaper.

___ I saw video of it on the Internet or TV.

___ I saw one myself.

___ A teacher at school says they could exist based on mathematical probabilities in the universe.

___ I got on board a UFO and flew around the world.

3. Pick one of the following stories to read: 1) Luke 24:13-24, 28-35; 2) John 20:10-18; or 3) John 10:24-31. Imagine you're a reporter for the local Jerusalem newspaper and you've interviewed the people in the story. Describe the following:

Whom did Jesus appear to?

What were their feelings before they encountered Jesus?

How did they know it was Jesus?

What did they believe about Jesus afterward?

4. Read 1 Corinthians 15:3-7. List the people Paul says Jesus appeared to after his resurrection.

5. When you think of what it means to be a Christian, which of the following images from the Bible are the most meaningful to you? Circle your top two.

Baptism	Lord's Supper/Eucharist	Washing feet	Jesus' healing
The cross	The empty tomb	Pentecost	The Good Shepherd

THIS WEEK

The resurrection of Jesus Christ was the culminating demonstration of God's power over sin and death. The accounts of those who first saw Jesus after his resurrection give us glimpses of how grief turned into joy when the reality of what had just happened set in for the early followers of Christ. The resurrection is not only a great story of something that happened in the past, but also a present reality for us today—that Jesus is alive and serves as our advocate. This TalkSheet takes students to those first appearances and connects them with the present reality that Christ has risen.

OPENER

Have students share what Easter traditions they remember from their childhoods. Try to get a full range of answers: Did they go to an early church service? Eat certain food? Hunt for eggs? Give gifts? Dress up? Ask what stories these events tell. The early witnesses to the resurrection told stories about it, some of which are in the Bible. Have three different students read Acts 2:1-12; 6:8-15; and 7:51-60. What's the main focus of these stories? What do these eyewitnesses teach us about Jesus' resurrection?

DISCUSSION

Before you begin: Be careful as you go through these first two discussion questions. This isn't about Jesus' appearances being similar to people seeing a UFO. Rather, it's about the testimonies of those who saw Jesus alive and their efforts to tell others about his resurrection.

1. Discuss how many of your students think UFOs exist, and try to get each to voice their reasons for their convictions one way or another. You may want to ask if anyone has proved they don't exist.

2. This is about proof. What does it take for your students to be convinced? Tell students that people today don't believe in Christ because they want proof. Which proof is most convincing? Do your students believe what they see on videos or on TV? Discuss with your students how they choose what to believe. Then transition to what it must have been like for those who saw Christ alive to try to prove to others that he had indeed risen from the dead.

3. This question takes a while to complete, so give students ample time to share. What feelings are present in the story? How were their lives changed because of their encounter with Christ? Where was the counter-testimony, the proof that Jesus *hadn't* risen from the dead?

4. Why was it important for Paul to list all these people? Do you think people were skeptical of the story? Read 1 Corinthians 15:14 to your students: "And if Christ has not been raised, our preaching is useless and so is your faith." Discuss with your students why the resurrection is important.

5. Have students share the ones that mean the most to them. All of them are important, so don't allow others to rank them in importance. Most Christians in America think of the cross as the important symbol in this list. Based on the TalkSheet discussion today, how might the empty tomb be an equally powerful symbol? How does the empty tomb give more power and meaning to what Christ did on the cross?

CLOSE

Quickly summarize the main points from the discussion, repeating the main things that were said by you and the students. Focus students' thinking on the empty tomb, reminding them of what it must have been like for those early believers as they tried to convince others of the reality that Jesus had risen from the dead. We take for granted that Jesus is alive, but those early believers were very sad, shocked, and scared.

MORE

• **There are many great resources online regarding the resurrection. Josh McDowell has done an extensive amount of work to equip youth workers and students with usable resources. He has a Web site on the resurrection at www.leaderu.com/everystudent/easter/articles/josh2.html. You can also check out more resources on his Web site at www.beyondbelief.com/r_apologetics.spl. If you want to use some of the apologetics' material, that would fit well with question #4.**

• **If you want to focus students more on what it must've been like for the early Christians, discuss how talking about a UFO sighting is similar or different from what the early Christians experienced when they shared what they saw at the empty tomb. To prompt discussion, there are some great UFO sighting stories online—one at Chicago O'Hare airport in 2006 and in Stephensville, Texas, in 2008—you can do a Google search and show them to students to discuss how we react to the unexpected.**

1. What does it mean to deny something? Write a definition for denial:

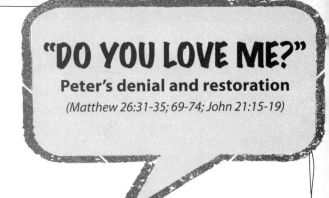

2. Get with two or three others around you and read about Peter's denials in Matthew 26:69-74. Pick one of the three times that Peter denied knowing Jesus and quickly draw below what you imagine that scene looked like.

Write down what your group thinks are one or two reasons Peter denied Jesus:

3. Read John 21:15-19, then read the following statements and decide if each one is "T" (True) or "F" (False).

_____ Peter's father's name was John.

_____ Jesus questions Peter three times.

_____ One of Jesus' commands to Peter is to feed the birds.

_____ When Jesus asked Peter if he loved him, Peter said no.

_____ Jesus questioned Peter after lunch.

_____ Peter's feelings were hurt when Jesus asked three times whether Peter loved him.

4. Describe a time when a parent, teacher, director, or coach encouraged you in front of other people. What did that feel like?

5. In your groups, have each person read out loud one of the following passages. Write down next to each one what Peter did to help start the early church.

Acts 2:37-42

Acts 4:8-15

Acts 10:44-48

THIS WEEK

Peter, the one God would build his church on, actually denied Jesus when the going got tough. Despite Peter's poor choices, he discovered Jesus was willing and able not only to forgive, but also to restore so that God could still use Peter. And in the end Peter became one of the most important leaders of the early church. This Talk-Sheet gives students the opportunity to understand that they, too, can be forgiven and used by God for his kingdom's purposes.

OPENER

Print Matthew 26:31-35 and Matthew 26:69-74 and choose two students beforehand to stand up and read these verses. Before handing out the TalkSheets to your students, let them know they'll be learning about how the Apostle Peter denied having known and been with Jesus—but also how Jesus later restored him.

For your opener, play a rousing game of To Tell the Truth. Hand out 3 x 5 cards the week before where students are to write things they've done in the past that no one else knows about, but that they'd be okay with people finding out about. Find one that works and see if that student would be willing to use it as part of the opener. Select two other students and meet with the three beforehand to go over the details. Have the three contestants come up and take seats. Each will try to fool the crowd, claiming to have done the same thing—but only one is telling the truth. Tell the group, "Only one of these people is telling the truth. They all claim to have done it—your job is to figure out which one is telling the truth." Let them ask any questions of all three or to a specific person. The three must answer as best they can to convince the crowd. After five minutes, stop and see who the group thinks is telling the truth, and then reveal it to them. How did they figure it out? How do we know when someone is telling the truth or denying it?

DISCUSSION

1. What definitions did your students create? The official definition is "refusal to satisfy a request or desire, refusal to admit the truth or reality, assertion that an allegation is false, or refusal to acknowledge a person or a thing." Which of these was Peter doing?

2. How did your students envision this scene? What were the facial expressions? The postures? Give each group a chance to give their reason for why Peter denied Jesus. This might be a point to discuss—whether middle school students have pressure on them to deny or hide the fact that they're Christians.

3. Have the students yell out the answer to each one. The answers are: T, T, F, F, F, and T. Make this as loud and fun as you want and clarify any questions they may have.

4. Luke 24:34 and 1 Corinthians 15:5 are the two verses that suggest Jesus appeared to Peter privately before he appeared to some of the others, probably the time when Jesus most likely offered forgiveness to Peter for his denials. Because of that, when Jesus publicly challenges Peter in John 21, it's to encourage those around to keep trusting in Peter (Matthew 16:18). Allow some time for students to share how an adult encouraged them publicly. If you have a large group, then do this in smaller groups so more kids can share.

5. Jesus said that Peter was the rock (Matthew 16:18), the foundation of the church—even though Jesus knew that Peter would later deny him. Remind students that Peter could be used in mighty ways for Christ, and that it's encouraging to know that no matter what we do, we can be forgiven and continue to be used by God in mighty ways.

CLOSE

This is not as much a story about Peter's denial as it is about his restoration. Jesus died on the cross for all our sins, and when we find forgiveness through him, we can be sure we've been forgiven and restored. Talk about the concept of restoration, and make sure your students have a clear idea of what that means.

Display the following verses using PowerPoint or a large board up front: 1 John 1:9, 2 Corinthians 5:17, and Galatians 2:20. Tell students you want them to memorize one of these three verses over the next week, so they need to be ready to write one of them down. Have three students with good voices stand up and each read a verse. Have students write down on their TalkSheet the reference that means the most to them. Challenge them to memorize that verse over the next week. Check for this on the following week.

MORE

• **What are ways we deny other people? Look at the definitions again and think of friends, family, parents, teachers, maybe ourselves. This is a great time for students to consider when they may have denied someone else—and to consider going to them and asking forgiveness. Discuss that with students: Is that something we should even consider? Is it too difficult? Why? You may want students to prayerfully consider who they need to write a note to or talk to, and to write that name on the TalkSheet.**

• **Ask your kids to look at some of the following verses about denial: Job 31:24-28; Matthew 10:33; Mark 8:38; 2 Timothy 1:8; 2:12; and Titus 1:16. What do these verses say about denial and our relationship with God? What does that mean for us today?**

(Thanks to Tom Carpenter for this TalkSheet idea)

1. **If I were asked to read something I like, it would be a (circle one letter):**

    A. Miracle I like to read about.

    B. Story with a deeper meaning.

    C. Poem that makes me feel good.

    D. Science fiction book.

    E. Story about an adventure or war.

    F. True story about history.

    G. Magazine.

    H. Sports story.

    I. Booklet of instructions for a video game.

2. **Which of the following best describes what you've learned about the end times (pick one)?**

    ❑ There will be a rapture of the church, then seven years of tribulation.

    ❑ Christ will come back after a time of tribulation and reign on earth for 1,000 years.

    ❑ Daniel and Revelation are symbolic and talk about the church age from Pentecost.

    ❑ The events of Revelation have happened in history and are happening now.

    ❑ All the signs of the end times have been fulfilled and we're waiting for Christ's return.

    ❑ I haven't ever really studied the end times and don't know much about it.

3. **Most middle schoolers are uncertain about the end times—what it would be like and whether you'd want to be there when it happens. Write down two questions you have about the end times.**

4. **Look up any two of the following passages and read them. Write down what they say will happen in the future.**

    Matthew 24:29-30—

    John 14:3—

    Acts 1:10-11—

    1 Thessalonians 2:19—

5. **Read the story in Matthew 25:1-13. In the story, what was the difference between being foolish and being wise?**

What does verse 13 mean as it relates to Jesus' return?

What should people do to prepare for Jesus' return?

THIS WEEK

End times is a topic middle school students like to study. It's mysterious and exciting, but there can also be a lot of fear and uncertainty. Throughout history, Christians looked with fascination at the events of the day, often convinced *they* were living in the end times. This session is a first look at some of the key biblical themes regarding the end times. This TalkSheet allows students to ask any question they have about end times, so plan to do a little background study or plan a second session to work through them.

OPENER

Ask students what images come to mind when you mention the phrase "the end times." Get as many quick responses as you can. This will reveal what your students know about end times as well as what feelings they may have. Tell students you're going to focus on the important biblical topic of end times. Ask students who are really into talking about end times to raise their hands. Have students who would say they try to avoid talking about the end times raise their hands. Ask those who are somewhere in the middle to raise their hands. Discuss with your students whether teenagers should even care to know about the end times. Is it okay to be really *into* it? Should they be scared about the end times?

DISCUSSION

1. Read through these and have students stand to indicate the one they selected. Ask some of the students who stood up to share why they picked that. If we prefer different kinds of reading material, is it possible to read the same thing (say, a poem) and get different meanings from it? Is it possible to do that with parts of the Bible? Do most of your friends even read the Bible at all? (Would that improve if you IMed or texted a verse a day to your friends?) Discuss what parts of the Bible your students have read and which parts they haven't—and why.

2. Each of these views represents a different way Christians interpret the Bible's writings about end times. Which of these seems the strangest to your students? Which one was the most popular with your students? Ask your students how they learned about the end times.

3. (Are you ready for this?) Ask students to volunteer the questions they wrote about the end times. Answer those you can and write down any you need to study or want to defer to a later time. You may want to bring in a trusted and knowledgeable adult or pastor to help with the tough ones. In fact, you may just want to have students write these on a separate paper to turn in for a potential second session.

4. All four of these passages declare that Jesus is coming again, an event described as something the whole world would experience. Ask your middle schoolers if they think about the fact that Jesus said he's coming back. What does the reality that Jesus is coming back and could come at any moment mean for them?

5. The wise ones were prepared, even though the bridegroom took a long time to arrive. As your students think about Jesus' coming again, what does it mean to be prepared? How should we be watching? Discuss how this story can also be applied to watching our life (actions) and our heart (affections).

CLOSE

The most basic and consistent truths about the end times are that (a) Jesus is coming back, (b) he could do so at any hour, and (c) it will be a universal and final event. Remind your students that throughout history, Christians have looked at events of their day and thought they were in the end times. Ask students to summarize what you talked about during this TalkSheet about the end times. Pause with students and have them imagine (but not answer out loud) that tonight is the night when Jesus comes back—how would they respond? What would Jesus say to them? Close with prayer and ask God to help you and your students live with an eternal perspective, not just live each day focused on our day-to-day concerns.

MORE

• **You may want to teach your students some of the major terms associated with the end times. Search for a "Jeopardy PowerPoint" online (Google it—there are many, so make sure you get one you can use effectively) and Google "end times" and "eschatology." You'll find various Web sites with terms and their definitions. Divide your group into three teams and play the game. You'll want to make sure that it's middle school-friendly (not too difficult) and it'll take some time because you'll want to teach as you move through this. It's a helpful and fun way to have students interact with major terms. Remember to encourage them to play as entire teams rather than just one outgoing student from each team.**

• **For more passages on end times, have students study Daniel 9:20-27; 12:1-4; Zechariah 14:1-5; Matthew 24:1-28; 2 Thessalonians 2:1-12; 1 John 2:18-19; and Revelation 20:1-10. If you're leading a church group, get a copy of your church's doctrine on end times to help your students see how these passages and others apply.**